POLICE CHAPLAINCY

The Role of the Police Chaplain, Supporting Officers, and Communities

Dr. Maxwell Shimba

Printed in the United States of America

TABLE OF CONTENTS

INTRODUCTION TO POLICE CHAPLAINCY

Police chaplaincy is a unique and essential component of law enforcement, providing spiritual and emotional support to officers, their families, and the community. Chaplains offer a compassionate presence and guidance in times of crisis, fostering a sense of hope and resilience within the force. This chapter explores the definition, history, and importance of police chaplaincy, laying the foundation for understanding its critical role in supporting those who serve and protect.

1.1 What is Police Chaplaincy?

Police chaplaincy involves trained and certified individuals who provide pastoral care, spiritual guidance, and emotional support to law enforcement officers and their families. These chaplains come from various religious backgrounds and are equipped to offer non-denominational support, respecting the diverse beliefs within the police force. Their role is to be a constant source of support, offering a listening ear, counseling, and guidance during both routine duties and critical incidents.

1.2 Historical Background

The concept of chaplaincy dates back centuries, with roots in military chaplaincy. Police chaplaincy began to take shape in the mid-20th century as law enforcement agencies recognized the need for spiritual and emotional support within their ranks. The first official police chaplaincy programs were established in the United States and have since spread globally, adapting to the specific needs and cultural contexts of different regions.

1.3 The Role of Faith in Law Enforcement

Faith plays a vital role in the lives of many officers, offering a source of strength and solace amidst the challenges of their profession. Police chaplains bridge the gap between faith and duty, ensuring that officers have the spiritual resources they need to perform their roles effectively. This support is crucial, as law enforcement officers often face high-stress situations, moral dilemmas, and exposure to traumatic events. Chaplains provide a safe space for officers to process their experiences and find spiritual grounding.

1.4 Importance of Police Chaplaincy

1.4.1 Emotional and Psychological Support

Law enforcement is a demanding profession that can take a toll on the mental health of officers. Police chaplains offer emotional and psychological support, helping officers cope with stress, anxiety, and trauma. This support is critical in preventing burnout and promoting overall well-being within the force.

1.4.2 Crisis Intervention

During crises, such as officer-involved shootings, accidents, or natural disasters, police chaplains are on the front lines, providing immediate support and comfort. Their presence helps stabilize situations and offers a source of hope and reassurance to those affected.

1.4.3 Building Trust and Morale

Chaplains help build trust and morale within the police force. By providing a non-judgmental and supportive presence, they foster a sense of community and solidarity among officers. This trust is essential for effective teamwork and the overall cohesiveness of the force.

1.4.4 Community Outreach

Police chaplains also play a crucial role in community outreach. They act as liaisons between the police force and the community, helping to bridge gaps and build positive relationships. Through faith-based initiatives and collaborative programs, chaplains promote understanding and cooperation between law enforcement and the communities they serve.

1.5 Case Studies and Impact

Real-life case studies highlight the profound impact of police chaplaincy. For instance, during the aftermath of the September 11 attacks, police chaplains provided critical support to officers and their families, helping them navigate the immense emotional and psychological toll. In another example, chaplains in a Midwest police department successfully implemented a peer support program, significantly reducing the rates of officer burnout and improving overall job satisfaction.

1.6 Challenges and Opportunities

While police chaplaincy is invaluable, it comes with its own set of challenges. Chaplains must navigate the complexities of maintaining confidentiality, balancing their dual roles as spiritual advisors and law enforcement supporters, and addressing the diverse spiritual needs within the force. Despite these challenges, the opportunities for growth and impact are immense. Continued training, interfaith collaboration, and community engagement can enhance the effectiveness of police chaplaincy programs.

1.7 Conclusion

Police chaplaincy is a vital aspect of law enforcement, providing indispensable spiritual and emotional support to officers, their families, and the community. By offering guidance and comfort in times of crisis, chaplains foster resilience and hope within the force. As law enforcement continues to evolve, the role of the police chaplain will remain crucial, adapting to meet the changing needs of those who serve and protect.

DR. MAXWELL SHIMBA

CHAPTER 01

HISTORICAL BACKGROUND

The Origins of Chaplaincy

The concept of chaplaincy has ancient roots, dating back to the early days of organized religion and warfare. Chaplains have historically provided spiritual support and guidance to soldiers, serving as a bridge between faith and the harsh realities of conflict. Their presence has been a source of comfort and moral support, helping to maintain the mental and spiritual well-being of those in combat.

Early Military Chaplaincy

The earliest recorded instances of military chaplaincy can be traced to the Roman Empire, where priests accompanied legions into battle, offering prayers and performing religious rituals. This tradition continued through the Middle Ages, with chaplains serving in the armies of various European kingdoms. During the Crusades, chaplains were integral to maintaining the morale of Christian soldiers, providing spiritual services and care for the wounded.

Evolution into Police Chaplaincy

The transition from military to police chaplaincy began in the 19th century as law enforcement agencies started to recognize the need for spiritual support within their ranks. The Industrial Revolution brought about significant social changes, leading to the formation of organized police forces in urban areas. These new police forces faced numerous challenges, including high levels of stress, exposure to violence, and public scrutiny. The need for a support system that addressed the spiritual and emotional well-being of officers became increasingly evident.

The Birth of Police Chaplaincy

The formal establishment of police chaplaincy can be traced back to the early 20th century in the United States. One of the earliest examples is the New York City Police Department, which appointed its first official chaplain in 1906. This move was driven by the recognition that officers needed more than just physical and tactical training; they required emotional and spiritual support to cope with the demands of their job.

Growth and Development

Throughout the 20th century, police chaplaincy programs expanded across the United States and other countries. The role of the police chaplain evolved to include not only spiritual guidance but also crisis intervention, counseling, and community outreach. Police chaplains became integral members of law enforcement agencies, offering support during critical incidents, such as officer-involved shootings, natural disasters, and terrorist attacks.

Key Milestones in Police Chaplaincy

1. World War I and II: The world wars highlighted the importance of chaplaincy in supporting military personnel. Many of the principles and practices developed in military chaplaincy were adapted for police chaplaincy, particularly in dealing with trauma and grief.

2. Civil Rights Movement: The 1960s and 1970s were a period of significant social upheaval in the United States. Police chaplains played a crucial role in mediating tensions between law enforcement and communities, promoting dialogue and understanding.

3. September 11, 2001: The terrorist attacks on September 11, 2001, marked a pivotal moment for police chaplaincy. Chaplains were on the front lines, providing immediate and long-term support to officers, their families,

and the community. Their work during this time underscored the vital role of chaplaincy in crisis response.

Global Expansion

The concept of police chaplaincy has spread globally, with many countries establishing their own programs. Each region has adapted chaplaincy to fit its cultural and religious contexts. In the United Kingdom, for example, police chaplaincy is integrated into the broader framework of emergency services chaplaincy, including fire and ambulance services. In Australia, police chaplains work closely with Indigenous communities, providing culturally sensitive support.

Modern Police Chaplaincy

Today, police chaplaincy is a well-established and respected component of law enforcement. Modern police chaplains are trained professionals who bring a diverse range of skills and experiences to their roles. They provide holistic support that addresses the spiritual, emotional, and psychological needs of officers and their families.

Challenges and Opportunities

While police chaplaincy has made significant strides, it faces ongoing challenges. These include addressing the diverse spiritual needs of officers, navigating the complexities of confidentiality and trust, and integrating chaplaincy services into increasingly secular societies. Despite these challenges, the opportunities for growth and impact are immense. Continued professional development, interfaith collaboration, and community engagement are key to the future success of police chaplaincy.

Conclusion

Understanding the historical evolution of police chaplaincy helps us appreciate its current significance and scope. From its ancient roots in military chaplaincy to its modern role in law enforcement, chaplaincy has consistently provided essential support to those in challenging and often dangerous professions. As police chaplaincy continues to evolve, its core mission remains the same: to offer spiritual and emotional support, fostering resilience and hope within the police force and the communities they serve.

This chapter has provided an overview of the historical background of police chaplaincy. Subsequent chapters will delve deeper into the specific roles and responsibilities of police chaplains, the types of chaplaincy services, and real-life stories that illustrate the profound impact of this essential vocation.

THE ROLE OF FAITH IN THE LAW ENFORCEMENT

1.1 Introduction

Faith plays a vital role in the lives of many law enforcement officers, providing a source of strength, solace, and guidance amidst the unique challenges they face daily. The presence of faith can significantly impact an officer's ability to cope with the stress, trauma, and moral complexities inherent in their profession. Police chaplains serve as a crucial bridge between faith and duty, ensuring that officers have access to the spiritual resources they need to perform their roles effectively.

1.2 The Importance of Faith for Law Enforcement Officers

Law enforcement officers operate in an environment characterized by high stress, potential danger, and exposure to traumatic events. The physical and emotional demands of the job can take a toll on their well-being, leading to burnout, mental health issues, and moral injury. Faith can provide a framework for resilience, offering officers a sense of purpose, hope, and moral grounding.

1.2.1 Resilience and Coping Mechanisms

Faith can enhance an officer's resilience by offering a sense of hope and optimism, even in the face of adversity. Belief in a higher power or a greater purpose can provide comfort and perspective, helping officers navigate the emotional aftermath of difficult situations. Prayer, meditation, and other spiritual practices can serve as coping mechanisms, reducing stress and promoting mental clarity.

1.2.2 Moral and Ethical Guidance

Law enforcement officers frequently encounter complex moral and ethical dilemmas. Faith can provide a moral compass, guiding officers in making decisions that align with their values and principles. This moral grounding can help officers maintain their integrity and uphold the ethical standards of their profession, even under pressure.

1.2.3 Community and Support

Faith-based communities offer a sense of belonging and support that can be invaluable to officers. These communities provide a network of individuals who share similar values and can offer encouragement, understanding, and practical assistance. Participation in faith-based activities can foster a sense of camaraderie and solidarity, reducing feelings of isolation.

1.3 The Role of Police Chaplains

Police chaplains play a pivotal role in integrating faith into the fabric of law enforcement. They provide spiritual and emotional support, counseling, and guidance to officers, their families, and the community. Chaplains ensure that officers have access to the spiritual resources they need, regardless of their religious affiliation or beliefs.

1.3.1 Spiritual Support and Counseling

Chaplains offer one-on-one spiritual support and counseling to officers, helping them process their experiences and emotions. They provide a safe and confidential space for officers to discuss their concerns, fears, and moral dilemmas. This support is tailored to the individual needs of each officer, respecting their beliefs and values.

1.3.2 Crisis Intervention

In times of crisis, police chaplains are often on the front lines, providing immediate spiritual and emotional support. Whether responding to officer-involved shootings, accidents, or natural disasters, chaplains offer comfort and guidance, helping officers and their families navigate the emotional aftermath. Their presence can help stabilize situations, providing a sense of calm and reassurance.

1.3.3 Conducting Ceremonies and Services

Police chaplains conduct a variety of ceremonies and services, including funerals, memorials, weddings, and invocations at official events. These ceremonies provide a sense of continuity and tradition, honoring the sacrifices and achievements of officers. Chaplains ensure that these events are inclusive and respectful of the diverse beliefs within the police force.

1.4 Faith in Action: Real-Life Examples

Real-life examples illustrate the profound impact of faith and chaplaincy in law enforcement. These stories highlight the ways in which faith provides strength, solace, and moral guidance to officers in their daily lives.

1.4.1 Officer Support during Traumatic Events

One powerful example involves a police officer who experienced a traumatic event while on duty. The officer was involved in a shooting that resulted in the loss of life. Struggling with guilt, fear, and emotional turmoil, the officer sought the support of a police chaplain. Through regular counseling sessions, prayer, and spiritual guidance, the chaplain helped the officer find peace and begin the healing process.

1.4.2 Community Healing after a Crisis

In another instance, a community faced a devastating natural disaster, resulting in widespread damage and loss of life. Police chaplains played a crucial role in the community's recovery, providing spiritual support to both officers and residents. They organized prayer vigils, offered counseling, and facilitated community gatherings that fostered a sense of hope and resilience.

1.5 Challenges and Considerations

While faith can be a powerful source of support, integrating it into law enforcement presents certain challenges and considerations. Police chaplains must navigate these complexities to ensure that their services are effective and inclusive.

1.5.1 Diversity of Beliefs

Law enforcement agencies are composed of individuals from diverse religious and spiritual backgrounds. Police chaplains must be sensitive to this diversity, providing support that is respectful and inclusive. This requires an understanding of different faith traditions and the ability to offer non-denominational support.

1.5.2 Maintaining Professional Boundaries

Chaplains must maintain professional boundaries, balancing their role as spiritual advisors with the need to respect officers' personal and professional lives. This includes ensuring confidentiality, avoiding proselytizing, and providing support in a manner that aligns with the ethical standards of the profession.

1.5.3 Addressing Secular and Non-Religious Needs

Not all officers identify with a particular faith or religion. Police chaplains must also be prepared to offer support to secular and non-religious officers, providing emotional and psychological care that respects their beliefs and values. This requires a holistic approach that encompasses spiritual, emotional, and mental well-being.

1.6 The Future of Faith in Law Enforcement

The role of faith in law enforcement is likely to continue evolving, reflecting broader societal changes and the diverse needs of officers. As police chaplaincy programs expand and develop, they will need to adapt to these changes, incorporating new approaches and resources to support officers effectively.

1.6.1 Training and Professional Development

Ongoing training and professional development are crucial for police chaplains to stay effective in their roles. This includes training in crisis intervention, counseling techniques, and cultural competency. Chaplains must also stay informed about the latest research and best practices in the field.

1.6.2 Interfaith Collaboration

Interfaith collaboration can enhance the effectiveness of police chaplaincy programs, providing a broader range of resources and perspectives. Partnerships with local religious organizations, community groups, and other chaplaincy programs can foster a more inclusive and comprehensive approach to support.

1.6.3 Embracing Technology

Technology offers new opportunities for police chaplaincy, from virtual counseling sessions to online resources for spiritual support. Embracing these technologies can help chaplains reach officers more effectively, particularly in remote or underserved areas.

1.7 Conclusion

Faith plays a vital role in law enforcement, offering a source of strength, solace, and moral guidance to officers as they navigate the challenges of their profession. Police chaplains serve as a crucial bridge between faith and duty, ensuring that officers have access to the spiritual resources they need to perform their roles effectively. By providing spiritual support, counseling, and crisis intervention, chaplains foster resilience and hope within the police force, contributing to the overall well-being and effectiveness of law enforcement agencies.

CHAPTER 02

BECOMING A POLICE CHAPLAIN

Qualifications and Training

To become a police chaplain, one must meet specific educational and experiential qualifications. This includes theological training, pastoral experience, and an understanding of the unique demands of law enforcement. This chapter will explore the essential qualifications, the training process, and the personal qualities required to be effective in this role.

2.1 Educational Qualifications

Educational qualifications for police chaplains generally include a combination of theological education and specialized training in pastoral care. While requirements can vary by jurisdiction and agency, most police chaplains possess the following credentials:

2.1.1 Theological Education

A solid foundation in theological education is crucial for police chaplains. This typically involves obtaining a degree from an accredited seminary, divinity school, or theological institution. Common degrees include:

- Bachelor of Theology (B.Th.)

- Master of Divinity (M.Div.)

- Doctor of Ministry (D.Min.)

These programs provide in-depth knowledge of religious texts, theology, ethics, and pastoral care. They also equip chaplains with the skills needed to offer spiritual guidance and support in a variety of settings.

2.1.2 Specialized Pastoral Training

In addition to theological education, aspiring police chaplains often undergo specialized training in pastoral care. This training focuses on the practical aspects of providing spiritual and emotional support, including:

- Clinical Pastoral Education (CPE): A program that combines classroom instruction with hands-on experience in clinical settings, such as hospitals, prisons, and counseling centers.

- Pastoral Counseling Certification: Certification programs that provide additional training in counseling techniques, crisis intervention, and ethical issues in pastoral care.

2.2 Experiential Qualifications

Experience in pastoral ministry and an understanding of the unique challenges faced by law enforcement officers are critical for effective police chaplaincy. Relevant experiences may include:

2.2.1 Pastoral Experience

Hands-on experience in pastoral ministry is essential. This can include serving as a pastor, minister, or priest in a religious congregation, where one gains experience in:

- Conducting religious services and ceremonies

- Providing spiritual counseling and guidance

- Supporting individuals and families through life events and crises

2.2.2 Law Enforcement Familiarity

Understanding the unique demands of law enforcement is crucial for police chaplains. This familiarity can be gained through:

- Ride-Alongs: Spending time with police officers during their shifts to gain firsthand experience of their work environment and challenges.

- Volunteer Work: Volunteering with law enforcement agencies in various capacities to build relationships and understand the culture.

- Continuing Education: Attending workshops, seminars, and courses focused on the intersection of law enforcement and pastoral care.

2.3 The Calling and Commitment

Becoming a police chaplain is more than just meeting educational and experiential qualifications; it requires a deep sense of calling and commitment. This section explores the personal qualities and motivations that are essential for effective police chaplaincy.

2.3.1 Sense of Calling

Many police chaplains describe their role as a calling—a deep-seated sense of purpose and vocation. This calling often stems from a desire to serve others, provide spiritual guidance, and support those in high-stress professions.

2.3.2 Compassion and Empathy

Compassion and empathy are fundamental qualities for police chaplains. The ability to listen without judgment, offer comfort, and understand the emotional and spiritual needs of others is crucial in building trust and providing effective support.

2.3.3 Resilience and Adaptability

The role of a police chaplain can be emotionally demanding and unpredictable. Resilience and adaptability are essential qualities, enabling chaplains to cope with stress, respond to crises, and provide steady support in a dynamic environment.

2.4 Certification and Licensing

Proper certification and licensing are crucial for police chaplains to operate effectively within the legal and ethical frameworks of law enforcement agencies. This section outlines the steps and requirements for obtaining these credentials.

2.4.1 Certification Programs

Various organizations offer certification programs for police chaplains. These programs ensure that chaplains meet the professional standards required for their role. Common certification programs include:

- International Conference of Police Chaplains (ICPC): Offers a comprehensive certification process, including training courses, workshops, and continuing education requirements.

- National Association of Chaplains to Law Enforcement (NACLE): Provides certification and resources for chaplains serving in law enforcement settings.

2.4.2 Licensing Requirements

Licensing requirements for police chaplains can vary by state and agency. Common requirements include:

- Background Checks: Ensuring that chaplains have a clean criminal record and are suitable for the role.

- Ethical Standards: Adhering to a code of ethics and professional conduct.

- Continuing Education: Participating in ongoing training and education to stay current with best practices and emerging trends in police chaplaincy.

2.5 Training Programs and Workshops

In addition to formal education and certification, police chaplains benefit from ongoing training programs and workshops. These programs enhance their skills and knowledge, ensuring they can effectively support law enforcement officers.

2.5.1 Crisis Intervention Training

Crisis intervention training equips chaplains with the skills to respond effectively to critical incidents, such as officer-involved shootings, accidents, and natural disasters. This training includes:

- Techniques for de-escalating tense situations

- Strategies for providing immediate emotional and psychological support

- Long-term follow-up care and support

2.5.2 Cultural Competency and Diversity Training

Police chaplains must be able to serve a diverse population, respecting and understanding various cultural and religious backgrounds. Cultural competency training helps chaplains:

- Develop awareness of different cultural and religious practices

- Provide inclusive and respectful support

- Navigate complex cultural dynamics within law enforcement agencies

2.6 Conclusion

Becoming a police chaplain requires a combination of educational and experiential qualifications, a deep sense of calling, and a commitment to ongoing professional development. Theological education, pastoral experience, and familiarity with law enforcement are foundational to this role. Certification, licensing, and specialized training ensure that chaplains can provide effective and ethical support to officers and their families.

This chapter has provided an overview of the qualifications and training required to become a police chaplain. Subsequent chapters will delve deeper into the specific roles and responsibilities of police chaplains, the types of chaplaincy services, and real-life stories that illustrate the profound impact of this essential vocation.

THE CALLING AND COMMITMENT

Introduction

Becoming a police chaplain is more than a job; it is a calling that requires dedication, compassion, and a genuine desire to serve those who protect and serve. This chapter explores the motivations and commitments necessary for this vocation, highlighting the personal qualities and spiritual convictions that drive individuals to become police chaplains. It delves into the unique challenges and rewards of the role, offering insights into what it truly means to be called to this important work.

2.1 Understanding the Calling

A calling is often described as a profound inner sense that one is meant to pursue a particular path or vocation. For police chaplains, this calling is rooted in a deep desire to provide spiritual and emotional support to law enforcement officers and their families. It involves a commitment to be present in times of crisis, to offer hope and encouragement, and to help officers navigate the moral and ethical complexities of their profession.

2.1.1 Spiritual Conviction

The calling to become a police chaplain is often grounded in strong spiritual convictions. Many chaplains feel a divine prompting or a sense of spiritual duty to serve those in law enforcement. This conviction provides a solid foundation for the resilience and dedication required in this role.

2.1.2 Compassion and Empathy

Compassion and empathy are central to the calling of a police chaplain. A genuine concern for the well-being of officers and their families drives chaplains to offer support and guidance. This compassion extends beyond the professional realm, touching the personal lives of those they serve.

2.2 Personal Qualities of a Police Chaplain

Certain personal qualities are essential for those who feel called to police chaplaincy. These qualities enable chaplains to effectively support officers and navigate the challenges of their role.

2.2.1 Emotional Resilience

Police chaplains often encounter traumatic and emotionally charged situations. Emotional resilience is crucial, allowing chaplains to remain steady and supportive even in the face of distressing events. This resilience helps them to be a calming presence for officers and their families.

2.2.2 Integrity and Trustworthiness

Integrity and trustworthiness are foundational qualities for police chaplains. Officers must feel confident that they can trust their chaplain with sensitive information and personal struggles. Maintaining confidentiality and acting with integrity fosters a sense of trust and safety.

2.2.3 Adaptability

The dynamic nature of law enforcement work requires chaplains to be adaptable. They must be prepared to respond to a variety of situations, from routine counseling sessions to critical incidents. Flexibility and the ability to think on their feet are essential.

2.3 Motivations for Becoming a Police Chaplain

The motivations for becoming a police chaplain are as diverse as the individuals who pursue this calling. However, several common themes emerge among those who are drawn to this vocation.

2.3.1 A Desire to Serve

At the heart of the calling to police chaplaincy is a desire to serve. This desire is often rooted in a commitment to help others, particularly those who dedicate their lives to protecting and serving the community. Chaplains are motivated by the opportunity to make a positive impact in the lives of officers and their families.

2.3.2 A Commitment to Social Justice

Many police chaplains are motivated by a commitment to social justice. They see their role as an opportunity to promote ethical behavior, fairness, and compassion within the law enforcement community. This commitment drives them to support officers in making morally sound decisions and to advocate for the well-being of all individuals.

2.3.3 Personal Experiences

Personal experiences can also play a significant role in motivating individuals to become police chaplains. Some chaplains have had previous careers in law enforcement, bringing a unique perspective and understanding to their role. Others may have been personally impacted by the work of police officers, inspiring them to give back through chaplaincy.

2.4 The Commitments of a Police Chaplain

The calling to police chaplaincy involves several key commitments. These commitments shape the daily work of chaplains and define their approach to supporting law enforcement officers.

2.4.1 Commitment to Presence

Being present is a fundamental commitment for police chaplains. This means being available and accessible to officers, whether during routine duties or in times of crisis.

Chaplains commit to showing up, offering a listening ear, and providing support whenever it is needed.

2.4.2 Commitment to Confidentiality

Confidentiality is a cornerstone of the chaplain-officer relationship. Police chaplains commit to maintaining the confidentiality of the information shared with them, creating a safe space for officers to express their concerns and seek guidance.

2.4.3 Commitment to Continued Learning

The field of police chaplaincy is constantly evolving, and chaplains must commit to continued learning. This involves staying informed about best practices, attending training sessions and workshops, and continually developing their skills to better serve the law enforcement community.

2.5 Challenges and Rewards

The calling to police chaplaincy comes with its own set of challenges and rewards. Understanding these can provide a realistic perspective on the demands and gratifications of the role.

2.5.1 Challenges

- Emotional Toll: The emotional demands of supporting officers through trauma and crisis can be significant. Chaplains must find ways to manage their own emotional health while being fully present for others.

- Navigating Boundaries: Balancing the professional and personal aspects of their role requires careful navigation. Chaplains must maintain appropriate boundaries while building trust and rapport.

- Cultural Sensitivity: Law enforcement agencies are diverse, and chaplains must be culturally sensitive and inclusive in their approach.

2.5.2 Rewards

- Making a Difference: One of the most rewarding aspects of police chaplaincy is the opportunity to make a positive difference in the lives of officers and their families. Knowing that their support can provide comfort and hope is deeply fulfilling.

- Building Relationships: Chaplains often form strong, meaningful relationships with officers and their families. These connections can be a source of mutual support and enrichment.

- Personal Growth: The challenges of police chaplaincy can also lead to significant personal growth. Chaplains often find that their work deepens their own faith and strengthens their resilience.

2.6 Conclusion

Becoming a police chaplain is a profound calling that requires dedication, compassion, and a genuine desire to serve those who protect and serve. The motivations and commitments necessary for this vocation are rooted in a deep sense of purpose and a commitment to making a positive impact. While the role comes with its challenges, the rewards of providing spiritual and emotional support to law enforcement officers and their families are immeasurable.

This chapter has explored the calling and commitment required to become a police chaplain. Subsequent chapters will delve deeper into the specific roles and responsibilities of police chaplains, the types of chaplaincy services, and real-life stories that illustrate the profound impact of this essential vocation.

CERTIFICATION AND LICENSING

Introduction

Proper certification and licensing are crucial for police chaplains to operate effectively within the legal and ethical frameworks of law enforcement agencies. Certification ensures that chaplains have the necessary training and qualifications, while licensing provides a formal recognition of their professional status. This chapter outlines the steps and requirements for obtaining these credentials, highlighting the importance of maintaining high standards of practice and adherence to ethical guidelines.

2.1 Understanding Certification and Licensing

Certification and licensing serve as a validation of a chaplain's qualifications, ensuring that they are equipped to provide spiritual and emotional support to law enforcement officers. These credentials help maintain professional standards and instill confidence in both the officers they serve and the agencies they work within.

2.1.1 Certification

Certification is a formal acknowledgment by a recognized professional body that a chaplain has met specific educational and experiential requirements. It typically involves completing a series of training programs, passing exams, and adhering to a code of ethics. Certification bodies often provide ongoing education and support to ensure that chaplains stay current with best practices.

2.1.2 Licensing

Licensing is a legal requirement in some jurisdictions, providing official authorization for chaplains to practice within a particular state or region. Licensing usually involves meeting additional regulatory requirements, including background checks and adherence to state-specific laws governing professional conduct and confidentiality.

2.2 Steps to Certification

The process of becoming a certified police chaplain involves several key steps. These steps ensure that chaplains are adequately prepared to meet the demands of their role and provide high-quality support to law enforcement officers.

2.2.1 Educational Requirements

The first step in becoming certified is to meet the educational requirements set by the certifying body. These requirements typically include:

- Theological Education: A degree from an accredited seminary, divinity school, or theological institution is often required. Common degrees include a Bachelor of Theology (B.Th.), Master of Divinity (M.Div.), or Doctor of Ministry (D.Min.).

- Pastoral Training: Additional training in pastoral care, such as Clinical Pastoral Education (CPE) or certification in pastoral counseling, is often required. This training provides practical experience in offering spiritual and emotional support.

2.2.2 Practical Experience

Practical experience in a pastoral role is crucial for certification. This experience can include serving as a pastor, minister, or priest in a religious congregation. It should involve:

- Conducting religious services and ceremonies

\- Providing spiritual counseling and guidance

\- Supporting individuals and families through life events and crises

2.2.3 Specialized Training

Specialized training in police chaplaincy is essential. This training focuses on the unique needs of law enforcement officers and includes:

\- Crisis Intervention: Techniques for providing immediate support during critical incidents

\- Ethics and Confidentiality: Understanding the ethical considerations and maintaining confidentiality in a law enforcement setting

\- Cultural Competency: Training in cultural sensitivity and diversity to effectively support a diverse police force

2.2.4 Certification Examination

Many certifying bodies require candidates to pass a certification examination. This exam tests knowledge of theological principles, pastoral care practices, and the specific demands of police chaplaincy. Preparation for the exam may involve studying relevant texts, attending workshops, and participating in study groups.

2.2.5 Continuing Education

Certification is not a one-time achievement; it requires ongoing education to maintain. Certified chaplains must participate in continuing education programs to stay current with best practices, new developments in pastoral care, and emerging trends in law enforcement support.

2.3 Certification Bodies

Several organizations provide certification for police chaplains. These bodies offer resources, training, and support to help chaplains meet the necessary standards.

2.3.1 International Conference of Police Chaplains (ICPC)

The ICPC is one of the leading organizations providing certification for police chaplains. It offers a comprehensive certification process that includes training courses, workshops, and continuing education requirements. The ICPC also provides a code of ethics and professional conduct guidelines.

2.3.2 National Association of Chaplains to Law Enforcement (NACLE)

NACLE provides certification and resources for chaplains serving in law enforcement settings. Its certification process includes educational and experiential requirements, as well as ongoing professional development opportunities.

2.4 Licensing Requirements

In addition to certification, some jurisdictions require police chaplains to obtain a license to practice. Licensing requirements vary by state and agency but generally include the following:

2.4.1 Background Checks

A thorough background check is typically required to ensure that the chaplain has a clean criminal record and is suitable for the role. This check may include:

- Criminal history

- Professional Conduct

- Verification of educational and experiential qualifications

2.4.2 Ethical Standards

Licensing bodies often require adherence to a code of ethics and professional conduct. This code ensures that chaplains maintain high standards of integrity, confidentiality, and respect in their interactions with officers and the community.

2.4.3 Continuing Education and Renewal

Licenses must be renewed periodically, which may involve completing additional continuing education requirements and demonstrating ongoing competence in the field. This ensures that chaplains remain up-to-date with best practices and new developments.

2.5 Importance of Certification and Licensing

Certification and licensing are essential for maintaining the professionalism and credibility of police chaplaincy. They ensure that chaplains have the necessary qualifications and adhere to ethical standards, providing confidence to the law enforcement agencies and officers they serve.

2.5.1 Professional Standards

Certification and licensing establish a baseline of professional standards that all chaplains must meet. These standards ensure that chaplains are well-trained, competent, and capable of providing high-quality support.

2.5.2 Ethical Practice

Adherence to ethical guidelines is crucial for maintaining trust and integrity in police chaplaincy. Certification and licensing bodies provide codes of ethics that guide chaplains in their interactions with officers, ensuring that they act with honesty, respect, and confidentiality.

2.5.3 Confidence and Credibility

Having certified and licensed chaplains enhances the credibility of the chaplaincy program within law enforcement agencies. Officers and their families can have confidence in the chaplain's qualifications and professionalism, making them more likely to seek and benefit from their support.

2.6 Conclusion

Proper certification and licensing are crucial for police chaplains to operate effectively and ethically within the framework of law enforcement agencies. These credentials ensure that chaplains are well-prepared to meet the demands of their role and provide high-quality support to officers and their families. By maintaining high standards of practice and adhering to ethical guidelines, certified and licensed chaplains can make a significant positive impact within the law enforcement community.

CHAPTER 03

ROLES AND RESPONSIBILITIES

Spiritual Support and Guidance

Police chaplains play a crucial role in providing spiritual support and guidance to law enforcement officers, helping them navigate both personal and professional challenges through faith-based support. This chapter explores the various ways chaplains offer spiritual counseling, the impact of their support, and the essential qualities that enable them to fulfill this role effectively.

3.1 The Scope of Spiritual Support

Spiritual support encompasses a broad range of activities and services aimed at addressing the spiritual and emotional needs of law enforcement officers. This support is not limited to any particular faith tradition; rather, it is inclusive and adaptable to the diverse beliefs of the officers.

3.1.1 One-on-One Counseling

One-on-one counseling sessions provide officers with a private and confidential space to discuss their concerns, seek guidance, and receive support. These sessions can address various issues, including:

- Stress and Anxiety: Helping officers manage job-related stress and anxiety through spiritual practices, meditation, and prayer.

- Moral and Ethical Dilemmas: Assisting officers in navigating complex moral and ethical decisions, reinforcing their values and principles.

- Personal Issues: Offering support for personal issues such as family problems, relationship difficulties, and grief.

3.1.2 Group Support and Workshops

Chaplains often conduct group support sessions and workshops that provide officers with opportunities to share experiences, learn coping strategies, and strengthen their sense of community. These activities can include:

- Peer Support Groups: Facilitating discussions among officers to promote mutual support and understanding.

- Workshops on Stress Management: Teaching techniques for managing stress, improving mental health, and maintaining spiritual well-being.

- Ethics and Values Training: Providing training on ethical decision-making and the integration of personal values into professional conduct.

3.1.3 Crisis Intervention

During critical incidents, police chaplains offer immediate spiritual and emotional support to officers and their families. Crisis intervention involves:

- On-Scene Support: Being present at the scene of traumatic events to provide comfort and reassurance to officers.

- Post-Incident Counseling: Offering follow-up counseling to help officers process their experiences and begin the healing process.

- Support for Families: Providing spiritual support and guidance to the families of officers affected by critical incidents.

3.2 The Impact of Spiritual Guidance

The spiritual guidance provided by police chaplains has a profound impact on the well-being of officers, their families, and the broader law enforcement community. This support contributes to:

3.2.1 Emotional Resilience

Spiritual support helps officers develop emotional resilience, enabling them to cope with the stresses and traumas of their job. This resilience is built through:

- Faith-Based Practices: Encouraging officers to engage in practices such as prayer, meditation, and reflection.

- Positive Outlook: Helping officers maintain a positive outlook and find meaning in their work, even in difficult circumstances.

- Supportive Relationships: Fostering a sense of community and connection through spiritual guidance and peer support.

3.2.2 Ethical Conduct

Chaplains play a vital role in promoting ethical conduct within law enforcement agencies. Through spiritual counseling, chaplains help officers:

- Clarify Values: Reinforce their personal and professional values, ensuring that their actions align with their ethical beliefs.

- Navigate Dilemmas: Provide guidance on how to handle ethical dilemmas and make morally sound decisions.

- Integrity and Accountability: Encourage officers to uphold integrity and accountability in their actions and interactions.

3.2.3 Overall Well-Being

The holistic approach of spiritual guidance addresses the overall well-being of officers, encompassing their physical, mental, and spiritual health. This comprehensive support includes:

- Mental Health Support: Addressing mental health issues through counseling and referrals to mental health professionals when necessary.

- Physical Health Promotion: Encouraging healthy lifestyle choices and self-care practices that contribute to overall well-being.

- Spiritual Growth: Supporting officers in their spiritual growth and development, helping them find deeper meaning and purpose in their lives.

3.3 Essential Qualities of Effective Police Chaplains

Effective police chaplains possess several essential qualities that enable them to provide meaningful spiritual support and guidance. These qualities include:

3.3.1 Compassion and Empathy

Compassion and empathy are fundamental qualities for police chaplains. They must be able to:

- Listen Actively: Listen to officers' concerns without judgment, offering understanding and support.

- Show Genuine Care: Demonstrate genuine care and concern for the well-being of officers and their families.

- Offer Comfort: Provide comfort and reassurance in times of distress, helping officers feel valued and supported.

3.3.2 Integrity and Confidentiality

Maintaining integrity and confidentiality is crucial for building trust and credibility with officers. Chaplains must:

- Adhere to Ethical Standards: Uphold high ethical standards in their conduct and interactions.

- Protect Privacy: Ensure that all discussions and counseling sessions remain confidential, fostering a safe space for officers to share their concerns.

- Build Trust: Establish and maintain trust through consistent, honest, and respectful interactions.

3.3.3 Cultural Sensitivity and Inclusivity

Police chaplains serve a diverse population and must be culturally sensitive and inclusive in their approach. This involves:

- Respecting Diversity: Respecting and valuing the diverse beliefs, backgrounds, and experiences of officers.

- Adapting Support: Adapting spiritual support and guidance to meet the unique needs of each individual.

- Promoting Inclusivity: Creating an inclusive environment where all officers feel welcome and supported, regardless of their faith or beliefs.

3.4 Case Studies and Real-Life Examples

Real-life examples illustrate the profound impact of spiritual support and guidance provided by police chaplains. These case studies highlight the ways in which chaplains make a difference in the lives of officers and their families.

3.4.1 Supporting an Officer through Personal Crisis

Officer John was experiencing significant personal challenges, including marital problems and the recent loss of a close family member. Feeling overwhelmed, he reached out to the police chaplain for support. Through regular counseling sessions, the chaplain helped John process his grief, navigate his marital issues, and find strength in his faith. John's emotional resilience improved, and he was able to regain a sense of balance and purpose in his life.

3.4.2 Providing Comfort after a Critical Incident

Following a critical incident involving a fatal shooting, the police chaplain was called to the scene to provide immediate support to the involved officers. The chaplain offered prayers, listened to the officers' concerns, and provided words of comfort and reassurance. In the days and weeks that followed, the chaplain continued to offer counseling and support, helping the officers cope with the emotional aftermath and begin the healing process.

3.4.3 Facilitating a Peer Support Group

Recognizing the need for mutual support among officers, the police chaplain established a peer support group. The group provided a safe space for officers to share their experiences, discuss challenges, and offer encouragement to one another. The chaplain facilitated the discussions, providing spiritual guidance and promoting a sense of camaraderie and community. The group became a valuable resource for officers, enhancing their emotional resilience and overall well-being.

3.5 Conclusion

Police chaplains play a vital role in providing spiritual support and guidance to law enforcement officers, helping them navigate personal and professional challenges through faith-based support. The impact of their work is profound, contributing to the emotional resilience, ethical conduct, and overall well-being of officers. Effective chaplains possess essential qualities such as compassion, integrity, and cultural sensitivity, enabling them to provide meaningful and inclusive support. Real-life examples highlight the significant difference that chaplains make in the lives of officers and their families.

CRISIS INTERVENTION COUNSELING

Introduction

Chaplains are often called upon during crises to provide immediate emotional and psychological support to officers and their families during traumatic events. Crisis intervention and counseling are critical components of a police chaplain's role, enabling them to offer comfort, stability, and guidance in the aftermath of distressing incidents. This chapter explores the nature of crisis intervention, the specific techniques and approaches used by chaplains, and the impact of their support on the well-being of law enforcement officers and their families.

3.1 Understanding Crisis Intervention

Crisis intervention involves providing immediate assistance and support to individuals experiencing a traumatic event or crisis. The goal is to help individuals stabilize emotionally, reduce the intensity of their distress, and begin the process of recovery. For police chaplains, crisis intervention is an essential aspect of their ministry, requiring them to be present and available whenever and wherever they are needed.

3.1.1 Types of Crises

Police chaplains respond to a wide range of crises, including:

- Officer-Involved Shootings: Providing support to officers involved in shootings, as well as to their colleagues and families.

- Line-of-Duty Deaths: Offering comfort and assistance to the families and colleagues of officers who have died in the line of duty.

- Accidents and Injuries: Assisting officers and their families after serious accidents or injuries.

- Natural Disasters: Providing support to officers and the community during and after natural disasters, such as hurricanes, floods, and earthquakes.

- Personal Crises: Helping officers navigate personal crises, such as divorce, illness, or the death of a loved one.

3.1.2 Goals of Crisis Intervention

The primary goals of crisis intervention are:

- Stabilization: Helping individuals regain a sense of control and stability in the immediate aftermath of a crisis.

- Emotional Support: Providing a compassionate and empathetic presence to alleviate emotional distress.

- Practical Assistance: Offering practical support and resources to address immediate needs and concerns.

- Long-Term Recovery: Facilitating the beginning of the recovery process and connecting individuals with ongoing support and counseling.

3.2 Techniques and Approaches

Effective crisis intervention requires a range of techniques and approaches tailored to the specific needs of the individuals involved. Police chaplains employ various strategies to provide immediate and effective support during crises.

3.2.1 Active Listening

Active listening is a fundamental technique in crisis intervention. It involves fully engaging with the individual, listening attentively to their concerns, and providing a supportive and non-judgmental presence. Key elements of active listening include:

- Empathy: Demonstrating understanding and compassion for the individual's feelings and experiences.

- Validation: Acknowledging the individual's emotions and validating their reactions to the crisis.

- Clarification: Asking open-ended questions to clarify the individual's concerns and needs.

3.2.2 De-escalation

De-escalation techniques are used to reduce the intensity of emotional distress and prevent situations from escalating further. These techniques include:

- Calm Communication: Speaking in a calm and reassuring tone to help individuals feel safe and supported.

- Physical Presence: Maintaining a non-threatening and supportive physical presence to provide comfort.

- Grounding Techniques: Using grounding techniques, such as deep breathing exercises, to help individuals manage their anxiety and regain control.

3.2.3 Providing Information and Resources

Providing accurate information and resources is crucial during a crisis. Chaplains offer practical assistance by:

- Offering Clear Information: Providing clear and accurate information about the situation and available resources.

- Connecting to Resources: Connecting individuals with additional support services, such as mental health professionals, support groups, and community resources.

- Follow-Up Care: Ensuring that individuals receive ongoing support and follow-up care to address their long-term needs.

3.2.4 Spiritual Support

Spiritual support is a key component of crisis intervention for police chaplains. This support includes:

- Prayer and Rituals: Offering prayers, religious rituals, and other spiritual practices to provide comfort and solace.

- Faith-Based Counseling: Providing faith-based counseling that aligns with the individual's beliefs and values.

- Hope and Resilience: Encouraging individuals to draw on their faith and spiritual beliefs to find hope and resilience in the face of adversity.

3.3 The Impact of Crisis Intervention

The support provided by police chaplains during crises has a profound impact on the well-being of officers, their families, and the broader law enforcement community. The benefits of effective crisis intervention include:

3.3.1 Emotional Stabilization

Immediate emotional support helps individuals stabilize and regain a sense of control in the aftermath of a crisis. This stabilization is essential for preventing long-term psychological distress and promoting recovery.

3.3.2 Reduced Psychological Trauma

Early intervention can significantly reduce the risk of long-term psychological trauma, such as post-traumatic stress disorder (PTSD). By addressing emotional distress promptly, chaplains help mitigate the impact of traumatic events.

3.3.3 Enhanced Resilience

Crisis intervention fosters resilience by providing individuals with the tools and support they need to cope with adversity. This resilience enables officers and their families to recover more quickly and effectively from traumatic events.

3.3.4 Strengthened Community

The presence of police chaplains during crises strengthens the sense of community within law enforcement agencies. Officers and their families feel supported and valued, enhancing their overall well-being and sense of belonging.

3.4 Case Studies and Real-Life Examples

Real-life examples illustrate the critical role of police chaplains in crisis intervention and counseling. These case studies highlight the positive impact of their support during some of the most challenging times.

3.4.1 Support After an Officer-Involved Shooting

Following an officer-involved shooting, the police chaplain was immediately called to the scene to provide support to the involved officer and their colleagues. The chaplain offered prayers, listened to the officers' concerns, and provided a calming presence. In the days that followed, the chaplain continued to offer counseling and support, helping the officers process their emotions and begin the healing process.

3.4.2 Assisting a Family After a Line-of-Duty Death

When an officer was killed in the line of duty, the police chaplain provided immediate support to the officer's family. The chaplain helped the family navigate the initial shock and grief, offering prayers and comforting words. The chaplain also assisted with funeral arrangements and provided ongoing counseling to the family, helping them cope with their loss and find a path forward.

3.4.3 Responding to a Natural Disaster

During a major natural disaster, the police chaplain was on the front lines, providing support to officers and the community. The chaplain offered emotional and spiritual support to those affected by the disaster, helped coordinate relief efforts, and provided practical assistance to officers and their families. The chaplain's presence and support were instrumental in helping the community recover and rebuild.

3.5 Essential Qualities for Crisis Intervention

Effective crisis intervention requires specific qualities and skills. Police chaplains must possess the following to provide meaningful support during crises:

3.5.1 Compassion and Empathy

Compassion and empathy are crucial for understanding and addressing the emotional needs of individuals in crisis. Chaplains must demonstrate genuine care and concern for the well-being of those they support.

3.5.2 Calmness and Composure

Maintaining calmness and composure in the face of crisis is essential for providing effective support. Chaplains must be able to manage their own emotions and remain steady and reassuring for those they are helping.

3.5.3 Effective Communication

Clear and effective communication is vital for providing accurate information and emotional support. Chaplains must be able to convey empathy, offer guidance, and provide practical assistance through their words and actions.

3.5.4 Flexibility and Adaptability

Crisis situations are often unpredictable and dynamic. Chaplains must be flexible and adaptable, able to respond to changing circumstances and meet the evolving needs of those they support.

3.6 Conclusion

Crisis intervention and counseling are critical components of a police chaplain's role, enabling them to offer immediate and effective support to officers and their families during traumatic events. Through active listening, de-escalation, providing information and resources, and offering spiritual support, chaplains help individuals stabilize emotionally, reduce psychological trauma, and enhance resilience. The impact of their work is profound, fostering a sense of community and well-being within law enforcement agencies.

This chapter has explored the essential aspects of crisis intervention and counseling provided by police chaplains. Subsequent chapters will delve deeper into other roles and responsibilities of police chaplains, including spiritual support, community outreach, and the unique challenges and rewards of this vital vocation.

CONDUCTION CEREMONIES AND SERVICES

Introduction

Police chaplains play a vital role in conducting various ceremonies and services, providing comfort and continuity through life's significant moments. These ceremonies range from weddings and funerals to memorial services and ceremonial events within the law enforcement community. This chapter explores the different types of ceremonies conducted by police chaplains, their importance, and the preparation and execution involved in each.

3.1 The Role of Ceremonies in Law Enforcement

Ceremonies and services conducted by police chaplains serve several important functions within the law enforcement community:

- Providing Comfort: Offering emotional and spiritual support during significant life events.

- Fostering Continuity: Creating a sense of continuity and tradition within the police force.

- Building Community: Strengthening the bonds among officers, their families, and the community.

- Honoring Sacrifices: Recognizing and honoring the sacrifices and achievements of officers.

3.2 Types of Ceremonies and Services

Police chaplains officiate a variety of ceremonies and services, each with its unique significance and requirements. The following sections detail the most common types of ceremonies conducted by police chaplains.

3.2.1 Weddings

Police chaplains often officiate weddings for officers and their families. These ceremonies are deeply personal and significant, marking the beginning of a new chapter in the couple's lives. Key aspects of officiating weddings include:

- Premarital Counseling: Providing premarital counseling to help couples prepare for their marriage, discussing topics such as communication, conflict resolution, and shared values.

- Ceremony Planning: Assisting the couple in planning the ceremony, including selecting readings, vows, and any religious or cultural rituals.

- Officiating the Ceremony: Conducting the wedding ceremony, ensuring it reflects the couple's beliefs and wishes.

3.2.2 Funerals

Funerals are a core responsibility for police chaplains, providing comfort and support to grieving families and colleagues. These services honor the life and legacy of the deceased, offering a space for mourning and remembrance. Key aspects of officiating funerals include:

- Meeting with the Family: Meeting with the family to discuss their wishes for the service, including any specific religious or cultural traditions.

- Service Preparation: Preparing the funeral service, including selecting readings, prayers, and music that reflect the deceased's life and beliefs.

- Conducting the Service: Officiating the funeral service with compassion and sensitivity, providing words of comfort and hope to those in attendance.

- Follow-Up Support: Offering ongoing support to the grieving family and colleagues, helping them navigate their loss.

3.2.3 Memorial Services

Memorial services are held to honor the memory of officers who have died, either in the line of duty or from other causes. These services provide an opportunity for the law enforcement community to come together in remembrance and solidarity. Key aspects of officiating memorial services include:

- Planning the Service: Collaborating with the police department and the deceased's family to plan the memorial service, ensuring it reflects the individual's life and contributions.

- Honoring the Deceased: Including elements such as eulogies, tributes, and moments of silence to honor the deceased's service and sacrifice.

- Providing Support: Offering emotional and spiritual support to those in attendance, helping them process their grief and find comfort in their shared memories.

3.2.4 Ceremonial Events

Police chaplains also participate in various ceremonial events within the law enforcement community. These events can include promotions, retirements, award ceremonies, and official departmental functions. Key aspects of officiating ceremonial events include:

- Opening and Closing Prayers: Offering invocations and benedictions to open and close the ceremonies, invoking a sense of reverence and solemnity.

- Speeches and Reflections: Delivering speeches or reflections that acknowledge the significance of the event and honor the individuals being recognized.

- Symbolic Acts: Participating in symbolic acts, such as the presentation of awards or the lighting of candles, to enhance the ceremony's meaning.

3.3 Preparation and Execution

The preparation and execution of ceremonies and services require careful planning, attention to detail, and a deep understanding of the needs and wishes of those involved. The following sections outline the key steps in preparing and conducting these events.

3.3.1 Initial Consultation

The initial consultation with the individuals or families involved is a critical first step in planning any ceremony or service. During this consultation, the chaplain:

- Gathers Information: Collects information about the individual's or family's wishes, including any specific religious, cultural, or personal preferences.

- Provides Guidance: Offers guidance on the structure and content of the ceremony, helping to ensure it meets their needs and expectations.

- Establishes Trust: Builds trust and rapport, creating a supportive and respectful environment for planning.

3.3.2 Planning the Ceremony

Planning the ceremony involves several key tasks, including:

- Selecting Elements: Choosing readings, prayers, music, and other elements that reflect the beliefs and wishes of those involved.

- Coordinating Logistics: Coordinating logistics such as the location, timing, and any necessary equipment or materials.

- Drafting the Order of Service: Drafting an order of service that outlines the sequence of events, ensuring a smooth and cohesive ceremony.

3.3.3 Conducting the Ceremony

On the day of the ceremony, the chaplain's role is to:

- Lead with Confidence: Lead the ceremony with confidence and poise, ensuring it proceeds smoothly and respectfully.

- Provide Comfort: Offer words of comfort and support, helping those in attendance feel at ease and connected.

- Maintain Flexibility: Be prepared to adapt as needed, responding to any unexpected changes or needs with flexibility and grace.

3.3.4 Follow-Up Support

Following the ceremony, police chaplains continue to provide support to those involved. This follow-up support includes:

- Checking In: Checking in with individuals and families to offer continued emotional and spiritual support.

- Providing Resources: Providing resources and referrals for additional support, such as counseling or support groups.

- Maintaining Connection: Maintaining a connection with the individuals and families, offering ongoing care and support as needed.

3.4 The Impact of Ceremonies and Services

The ceremonies and services conducted by police chaplains have a profound impact on the individuals and communities they serve. These events:

3.4.1 Foster Healing

Funerals, memorial services, and other ceremonies provide a space for mourning and remembrance, fostering healing and closure for those who have experienced loss.

3.4.2 Strengthen Community

Ceremonial events strengthen the sense of community within the law enforcement family, bringing people together in shared experiences of celebration, remembrance, and honor.

3.4.3 Honor Traditions

Ceremonies and services honor the traditions and values of the law enforcement community, reinforcing a sense of continuity and pride.

3.4.4 Provide Comfort

By providing spiritual and emotional support during significant life events, police chaplains offer comfort and solace to officers and their families, helping them navigate both joyful and challenging times.

3.5 Case Studies and Real-Life Examples

Real-life examples illustrate the significant role of police chaplains in conducting ceremonies and services. These case studies highlight the ways in which chaplains provide comfort, honor, and continuity through their work.

3.5.1 A Wedding Ceremony for an Officer

Officer Sarah and her fiancé, Mark, wanted a wedding ceremony that reflected their faith and commitment to each other. The police chaplain provided premarital counseling, helping them prepare for their marriage. On the day of the wedding, the chaplain officiated a beautiful ceremony that included personalized vows, meaningful readings, and a heartfelt blessing. The couple and their guests felt deeply moved and supported by the chaplain's presence and guidance.

3.5.2 A Funeral for a Fallen Officer

When Officer James was killed in the line of duty, the police chaplain worked closely with his family to plan a funeral service that honored his life and service. The chaplain provided emotional support to the grieving family, helped them select meaningful readings and music, and officiated the service with compassion and dignity. The funeral was a powerful tribute to Officer James, offering comfort to his family and colleagues and reinforcing the sense of community within the department.

3.5.3 A Memorial Service for Retired Officers

The police department wanted to honor retired officers who had passed away over the past year. The police chaplain organized a memorial service that included tributes from colleagues, a roll call of the fallen officers, and a candle-lighting ceremony. The chaplain's words of remembrance and hope provided solace to the families and colleagues of the deceased, fostering a sense of continuity and gratitude within the law enforcement community.

3.6 Essential Qualities for Conducting Ceremonies

Conducting ceremonies and services requires specific qualities and skills. Police chaplains must possess the following to provide meaningful and impactful ceremonies:

3.6.1 Compassion and Empathy

Compassion and empathy are crucial for understanding and addressing the emotional needs of those involved in the ceremony. Chaplains must demonstrate genuine care and concern for the individuals and families they serve.

3.6.2 Organizational Skills

Strong organizational skills are essential for planning and coordinating ceremonies. Chaplains must be able to manage logistics, coordinate with multiple parties, and ensure that all elements of the ceremony come together smoothly.

3.6.3 Communication Skills

Effective communication skills are vital for conveying empathy, offering guidance, and leading ceremonies with clarity and confidence. Chaplains must be able to articulate their thoughts and emotions in a way that resonates with those in attendance.

3.6

.4 Cultural Sensitivity

Cultural sensitivity is important for conducting inclusive ceremonies that respect the diverse beliefs and traditions of the law enforcement community. Chaplains must be aware of and responsive to the cultural and religious backgrounds of those they serve.

3.7 Conclusion

Conducting ceremonies and services is a vital aspect of a police chaplain's role, providing comfort and continuity through life's significant moments. Whether officiating weddings, funerals, memorial services, or ceremonial events, chaplains offer emotional and spiritual support, honor traditions, and strengthen the sense of community within law enforcement. By demonstrating compassion, empathy, organizational skills, and cultural sensitivity, chaplains create meaningful and impactful ceremonies that resonate with those they serve.

This chapter has explored the various ceremonies and services conducted by police chaplains, their importance, and the preparation and execution involved in each. Subsequent chapters will delve deeper into other roles and responsibilities of police chaplains, including spiritual support, crisis intervention, and the unique challenges and rewards of this essential vocation.

BUILDING TRUST WITHIN THE FORCE

Introduction

Establishing and maintaining trust is a fundamental aspect of police chaplaincy, enabling chaplains to be effective confidants and advisors to officers. Trust forms the foundation for meaningful relationships, allowing chaplains to provide the necessary support and guidance to law enforcement personnel. This chapter explores the importance of building trust within the force, the strategies chaplains use to cultivate trust, and the impact of a trust-based relationship on the overall well-being of officers.

3.1 The Importance of Trust

Trust is essential for the effective functioning of any organization, particularly within law enforcement agencies where the stakes are high, and the stress levels are significant. Trust in police chaplains is crucial for several reasons:

3.1.1 Confidentiality and Safety

Officers must feel confident that their conversations with chaplains will remain confidential. This sense of safety encourages them to open up about personal and professional challenges without fear of judgment or repercussions.

3.1.2 Emotional Support

Trust allows officers to seek emotional support and counseling from chaplains, knowing that they will receive compassionate and non-judgmental assistance. This support is vital for managing stress, anxiety, and trauma.

3.1.3 Ethical Guidance

Chaplains often provide ethical and moral guidance. Trust ensures that officers will consider and respect the chaplain's advice when facing difficult decisions.

3.1.4 Community Building

Building trust fosters a sense of community and camaraderie within the force. It strengthens the bonds between officers and chaplains, enhancing the overall morale and cohesion of the department.

3.2 Strategies for Building Trust

Building trust within the force requires intentional effort and consistent behavior from police chaplains. The following strategies are essential for cultivating trust:

3.2.1 Demonstrating Consistency

Consistency in behavior and availability is crucial for building trust. Chaplains must:

- Be Reliable: Keep commitments and be available when needed.

- Act with Integrity: Uphold ethical standards and act with honesty and transparency.

- Show Commitment: Demonstrate a genuine commitment to the well-being of officers and their families.

3.2.2 Maintaining Confidentiality

Confidentiality is the cornerstone of trust. Chaplains must:

- Protect Privacy: Ensure that all conversations and counseling sessions are confidential.

- Respect Boundaries: Understand and respect the boundaries of personal information shared by officers.

- Build Safe Spaces: Create an environment where officers feel safe to express their concerns and emotions.

3.2.3 Active Listening

Active listening is a powerful tool for building trust. Chaplains must:

- Be Present: Give full attention to the officer, showing that their concerns are valued.

- Show Empathy: Demonstrate understanding and compassion for the officer's experiences.

- Respond Thoughtfully: Provide thoughtful and supportive responses that reflect a genuine concern for the officer's well-being.

3.2.4 Being Visible and Accessible

Visibility and accessibility are key to building trust. Chaplains must:

- Be Present: Spend time in the field, attending roll calls, and participating in department activities.

- Be Approachable: Make themselves approachable and available for informal conversations.

- Build Relationships: Engage with officers regularly to build rapport and establish trust-based relationships.

3.2.5 Providing Non-Judgmental Support

Non-judgmental support fosters trust and openness. Chaplains must:

- Avoid Judgment: Refrain from passing judgment on officers' actions or decisions.

- Offer Support: Provide unconditional support and understanding, regardless of the circumstances.

- Encourage Open Communication: Create an atmosphere where officers feel comfortable sharing their thoughts and feelings.

3.3 The Impact of Trust-Based Relationships

Trust-based relationships between police chaplains and officers have a profound impact on the overall well-being and effectiveness of the force. These relationships:

3.3.1 Enhance Emotional Well-Being

Trust-based relationships provide officers with a reliable source of emotional support. Chaplains help officers manage stress, anxiety, and trauma, contributing to their overall emotional well-being.

3.3.2 Improve Job Performance

Officers who feel supported and valued are more likely to perform their duties effectively. Trust in chaplains can lead to increased job satisfaction, better decision-making, and enhanced performance.

3.3.3 Foster Resilience

Trust-based relationships foster resilience by providing officers with the tools and support they need to cope with adversity. Chaplains help officers build emotional and psychological resilience, enabling them to recover more quickly from traumatic events.

3.3.4 Strengthen Community

Trust enhances the sense of community within the force. Officers who trust their chaplains are more likely to seek support, participate in community-building activities, and contribute to a positive and cohesive work environment.

3.4 Case Studies and Real-Life Examples

Real-life examples illustrate the importance and impact of trust-based relationships between police chaplains and officers. These case studies highlight the ways in which chaplains build trust and provide essential support.

3.4.1 Building Trust through Consistency

Officer Mike was initially skeptical about the role of the police chaplain. However, over time, he observed the chaplain's consistent presence at roll calls, departmental meetings, and in the field. The chaplain's reliability and commitment to the officers' well-being gradually built trust. When Mike experienced a personal crisis, he felt comfortable seeking the chaplain's support, knowing that he could rely on their confidentiality and non-judgmental approach.

3.4.2 Maintaining Confidentiality

Sergeant Laura faced a challenging ethical dilemma at work and was unsure how to proceed. She reached out to the police chaplain, who assured her that their conversation would remain confidential. The chaplain's respect for confidentiality allowed Laura to discuss her concerns openly and seek guidance. The trust she placed in the chaplain's discretion enabled her to make a decision that aligned with her values and the department's ethical standards.

3.4.3 Active Listening and Empathy

During a particularly stressful period, Officer Sam felt overwhelmed and isolated. The police chaplain noticed Sam's distress and took the time to engage in a one-on-one conversation. Through active listening and empathetic responses, the chaplain created a safe space for Sam to express his feelings. This interaction helped Sam feel understood and supported, improving his emotional well-being and reinforcing his trust in the chaplain's support.

3.5 Essential Qualities for Building Trust

Effective trust-building requires specific qualities and skills. Police chaplains must possess the following to establish and maintain trust within the force:

3.5.1 Integrity

Integrity is fundamental to trust-building. Chaplains must consistently act with honesty, transparency, and ethical behavior, ensuring that officers can rely on their word and actions.

3.5.2 Empathy

Empathy allows chaplains to connect with officers on a deeper level. By understanding and sharing the feelings of others, chaplains can provide meaningful support and build trust-based relationships.

3.5.3 Confidentiality

Maintaining confidentiality is crucial for trust. Chaplains must protect the privacy of the information shared with them, ensuring that officers feel safe to open up without fear of judgment or repercussions.

3.5.4 Reliability

Reliability builds trust through consistent and dependable behavior. Chaplains must be present, available, and committed to the well-being of officers, demonstrating that they can be counted on in times of need.

3.6 Conclusion

Building trust within the force is a fundamental aspect of police chaplaincy, enabling chaplains to be effective confidants and advisors to officers. Trust forms the foundation for meaningful relationships, allowing chaplains to provide the necessary support and guidance to law enforcement personnel. Through strategies such as demonstrating consistency, maintaining confidentiality, active listening, being visible and accessible, and providing non-judgmental support, chaplains cultivate trust-based relationships that enhance the emotional well-being, job performance, and resilience of officers.

CHAPTER 04

VOLUNTEER CHAPLAINS

Many police chaplains serve on a volunteer basis, dedicating their time and resources to support the force without financial compensation. These volunteer chaplains play a crucial role in providing spiritual and emotional support to law enforcement officers, their families, and the broader community. This chapter explores the unique contributions of volunteer chaplains, the motivations behind their service, the challenges they face, and the impact of their work on the police force and the community.

4.1 The Role of Volunteer Chaplains

Volunteer chaplains perform a wide range of duties, often mirroring those of their paid counterparts. Their responsibilities include providing spiritual counseling, crisis intervention, conducting ceremonies, and offering support during critical incidents. Despite not receiving financial compensation, volunteer chaplains are dedicated to serving the law enforcement community with the same level of commitment and professionalism.

4.1.1 Spiritual Counseling

Volunteer chaplains offer spiritual counseling to officers and their families, helping them navigate personal and professional challenges. This counseling includes:

- One-on-One Sessions: Providing individual counseling to address personal concerns, stress, and emotional well-being.

- Group Support: Facilitating support groups for officers to share experiences and offer mutual support.

- Faith-Based Guidance: Offering faith-based advice and support tailored to the individual's beliefs and values.

4.1.2 Crisis Intervention

In times of crisis, volunteer chaplains provide immediate support to officers and their families. This includes:

- On-Scene Support: Responding to critical incidents to offer comfort and reassurance.

- Follow-Up Care: Providing ongoing support and counseling after a crisis to help individuals process their experiences.

- Resource Referral: Connecting officers and their families with additional resources, such as mental health professionals and support groups.

4.1.3 Conducting Ceremonies

Volunteer chaplains officiate various ceremonies, including:

- Weddings: Conducting wedding ceremonies for officers and their families.

- Funerals and Memorial Services: Leading funeral and memorial services to honor fallen officers and provide comfort to grieving families.

- Departmental Events: Participating in promotions, retirements, and other ceremonial events within the department.

4.1.4 Community Engagement

Volunteer chaplains also engage with the broader community, fostering positive relationships between law enforcement and the public. This includes:

- Public Outreach: Participating in community events and activities to build trust and understanding.

- Educational Programs: Leading workshops and seminars on topics such as stress management, ethics, and resilience.

- Interfaith Collaboration: Working with religious and community leaders to promote inclusivity and support within the community.

4.2 Motivations for Volunteering

The motivations behind volunteering as a police chaplain are varied and deeply personal. Understanding these motivations provides insight into the dedication and commitment of volunteer chaplains.

4.2.1 Sense of Calling

Many volunteer chaplains feel a strong sense of calling or vocation, believing that they are divinely inspired to serve in this capacity. This sense of purpose drives their commitment to providing spiritual and emotional support to law enforcement officers.

4.2.2 Desire to Serve

A desire to serve the community and support those who protect and serve is a common motivation for volunteer chaplains. This altruistic desire to make a positive impact fuels their dedication to the role.

4.2.3 Personal Connections

Some volunteer chaplains have personal connections to law enforcement, such as family members or friends who are officers. These connections often inspire them to offer their support and expertise to the police force.

4.2.4 Professional Experience

Volunteer chaplains may have backgrounds in ministry, counseling, or social work, bringing valuable professional experience to their role. Volunteering allows them to apply their skills in a meaningful way, supporting the well-being of officers and their families.

4.3 Challenges Faced by Volunteer Chaplains

While volunteer chaplains provide invaluable support, they also face unique challenges. Understanding these challenges helps to appreciate the dedication and resilience required for this role.

4.3.1 Time and Resource Constraints

Balancing volunteer responsibilities with other personal and professional commitments can be challenging. Volunteer chaplains often have to manage their time effectively to fulfill their duties without neglecting other areas of their lives.

4.3.2 Lack of Financial Compensation

Serving without financial compensation can be a barrier for some individuals. Volunteer chaplains must find ways to sustain their involvement despite the lack of financial incentives.

4.3.3 Emotional Toll

The emotional demands of providing support during crises and critical incidents can take a toll on volunteer chaplains. They must develop strategies for self-care and resilience to manage the emotional impact of their work.

4.3.4 Access to Training and Resources

Volunteer chaplains may have limited access to training and resources compared to their paid counterparts. Ensuring that volunteer chaplains receive adequate training and support is essential for their effectiveness and well-being.

4.4 The Impact of Volunteer Chaplains

Despite the challenges, volunteer chaplains have a profound impact on the law enforcement community. Their dedication and service contribute significantly to the well-being of officers, their families, and the community.

4.4.1 Enhancing Officer Well-Being

Volunteer chaplains play a crucial role in enhancing the emotional and spiritual well-being of officers. Their support helps officers manage stress, cope with trauma, and maintain their mental health.

4.4.2 Strengthening Community Ties

By engaging with the community, volunteer chaplains help to build positive relationships between law enforcement and the public. Their efforts promote trust, understanding, and collaboration, fostering a stronger, more cohesive community.

4.4.3 Providing Continuity

Volunteer chaplains provide continuity in support, offering a consistent presence that officers can rely on during times of need. This continuity helps to build trust and strengthen the chaplain-officer relationship.

4.4.4 Encouraging Resilience

Through their counseling and support, volunteer chaplains help officers develop resilience, enabling them to recover more effectively from stress and trauma. This resilience is essential for the long-term well-being and effectiveness of the force.

4.5 Case Studies and Real-Life Examples

Real-life examples illustrate the significant contributions of volunteer chaplains to the law enforcement community. These case studies highlight the ways in which volunteer chaplains provide essential support and make a positive impact.

4.5.1 Supporting an Officer through Personal Crisis

Officer David was struggling with the recent loss of a family member, affecting his performance and well-being. The volunteer chaplain reached out to offer support, providing one-on-one counseling sessions. Through active listening and compassionate guidance, the chaplain helped David navigate his grief and regain a sense of stability and purpose.

4.5.2 Providing Comfort after a Critical Incident

Following a critical incident involving multiple casualties, the volunteer chaplain was on the scene to provide immediate emotional support to the affected officers. The chaplain offered prayers, comforting words, and practical assistance, helping the officers process their emotions and begin the healing process. The chaplain's presence provided a source of strength and reassurance during a challenging time.

4.5.3 Engaging with the Community

The volunteer chaplain organized a community outreach event to promote positive relationships between law enforcement and local residents. The event included educational workshops, interactive activities, and opportunities for officers and community members to connect. The chaplain's efforts helped to build trust and foster a sense of collaboration, enhancing the overall relationship between the police force and the community.

4.6 Essential Qualities for Volunteer Chaplains

Volunteer chaplains must possess specific qualities and skills to effectively fulfill their role. These qualities include:

4.6.1 Compassion

Compassion is essential for understanding and addressing the emotional needs of officers and their families. Volunteer chaplains must demonstrate genuine care and concern for those they serve.

4.6.2 Commitment

A strong commitment to the role is crucial for volunteer chaplains, given the demands and challenges of their work. This commitment drives their dedication to providing consistent and reliable support.

4.6.3 Flexibility

Flexibility is important for managing the varied and unpredictable nature of volunteer chaplaincy. Volunteer chaplains must be able to adapt to changing circumstances and respond to diverse needs.

4.6.4 Professionalism

Professionalism ensures that volunteer chaplains uphold high standards of conduct and integrity. This professionalism fosters trust and respect within the law enforcement community.

4.7 Conclusion

Volunteer chaplains play a vital role in supporting the law enforcement community, dedicating their time and resources to provide spiritual and emotional support without financial compensation. Their contributions enhance the well-being of officers, strengthen community ties, and promote resilience. Despite the challenges they face, volunteer chaplains demonstrate remarkable dedication and commitment, making a profound impact on the police force and the broader community.

This chapter has explored the unique contributions, motivations, challenges, and impact of volunteer chaplains. Subsequent chapters will delve deeper into other types of police chaplains, including part-time and full-time chaplains, and the specific roles and responsibilities they fulfill within the law enforcement community.

PART-TIME CHAPLAINS

Part-time chaplains balance their duties with other professional responsibilities, offering flexibility and adaptability in their service. This chapter explores the unique contributions of part-time chaplains, the benefits of their role, the challenges they face, and the strategies they use to effectively support the law enforcement community while managing their dual responsibilities.

4.1 The Role of Part-Time Chaplains

Part-time chaplains perform many of the same duties as full-time and volunteer chaplains, providing spiritual and emotional support to law enforcement officers and their families. Their responsibilities include spiritual counseling, crisis intervention, conducting ceremonies, and engaging with the community. However, their part-time status allows them to balance these duties with other professional or personal commitments.

4.1.1 Spiritual Counseling

Part-time chaplains offer spiritual counseling to officers and their families, helping them navigate personal and professional challenges. This counseling includes:

- Individual Counseling: Providing one-on-one support to address personal concerns, stress, and emotional well-being.

- Group Sessions: Facilitating group support sessions for officers to share experiences and offer mutual support.

- Faith-Based Guidance: Offering faith-based advice and support tailored to the individual's beliefs and values.

4.1.2 Crisis Intervention

Part-time chaplains provide immediate support during crises, including:

- On-Scene Response: Responding to critical incidents to offer comfort and reassurance.

- Follow-Up Support: Providing ongoing counseling and support after a crisis to help individuals process their experiences.

- Resource Connection: Connecting officers and their families with additional resources, such as mental health professionals and support groups.

4.1.3 Conducting Ceremonies

Part-time chaplains officiate various ceremonies, including:

- Weddings: Conducting wedding ceremonies for officers and their families.

- Funerals and Memorial Services: Leading funeral and memorial services to honor fallen officers and provide comfort to grieving families.

- Departmental Events: Participating in promotions, retirements, and other ceremonial events within the department.

4.1.4 Community Engagement

Part-time chaplains engage with the broader community to foster positive relationships between law enforcement and the public. This includes:

- Public Outreach: Participating in community events and activities to build trust and understanding.

- Educational Programs: Leading workshops and seminars on topics such as stress management, ethics, and resilience.

- Interfaith Collaboration: Working with religious and community leaders to promote inclusivity and support within the community.

4.2 Benefits of Part-Time Chaplains

Part-time chaplains offer several benefits to the law enforcement community due to their unique position and flexibility.

4.2.1 Flexibility

Part-time chaplains can offer flexible support, adjusting their availability to meet the needs of the department. This flexibility allows them to respond to urgent situations and provide ongoing support while balancing other commitments.

4.2.2 Diverse Perspectives

Balancing multiple roles allows part-time chaplains to bring diverse perspectives and experiences to their work. Their varied backgrounds can enrich their approach to counseling and support, benefiting the officers they serve.

4.2.3 Professional Skills

Part-time chaplains often possess professional skills and expertise from their other roles, which can enhance their effectiveness as chaplains. For example, experience in counseling, social work, or ministry can provide valuable insights and techniques for supporting officers.

4.2.4 Reduced Burnout

Part-time chaplaincy can help reduce the risk of burnout by allowing chaplains to maintain a balance between their duties and personal or professional lives. This balance can lead to greater job satisfaction and long-term commitment to the role.

4.3 Challenges Faced by Part-Time Chaplains

Despite the benefits, part-time chaplains face unique challenges in balancing their dual responsibilities. Understanding these challenges is essential for appreciating their dedication and resilience.

4.3.1 Time Management

Balancing the demands of chaplaincy with other professional or personal responsibilities requires effective time management. Part-time chaplains must prioritize tasks and manage their schedules to fulfill their duties effectively.

4.3.2 Availability

Part-time chaplains may face limitations in their availability, making it challenging to respond to emergencies or provide consistent support. They must find ways to remain accessible and responsive while managing other commitments.

4.3.3 Integration

Integrating into the law enforcement community as a part-time chaplain can be challenging. Building trust and rapport with officers may take longer due to their limited presence and availability.

4.3.4 Maintaining Boundaries

Maintaining professional boundaries while balancing multiple roles can be complex. Part-time chaplains must navigate the potential overlap between their chaplaincy duties and other professional responsibilities.

4.4 Strategies for Effective Service

Part-time chaplains use various strategies to effectively manage their dual responsibilities and provide meaningful support to the law enforcement community.

4.4.1 Prioritizing Tasks

Effective prioritization is crucial for managing multiple responsibilities. Part-time chaplains must identify the most critical tasks and allocate their time and resources accordingly.

4.4.2 Effective Communication

Maintaining open and effective communication with the department and officers is essential. Part-time chaplains must keep lines of communication open, ensuring they are accessible and responsive to the needs of the force.

4.4.3 Building a Support Network

Building a support network within the department can enhance the effectiveness of part-time chaplains. Collaborating with full-time chaplains, volunteers, and other support personnel can provide additional resources and coverage.

4.4.4 Continuous Professional Development

Part-time chaplains must engage in continuous professional development to stay current with best practices and enhance their skills. Attending training sessions, workshops, and conferences can provide valuable insights and techniques.

4.5 The Impact of Part-Time Chaplains

Part-time chaplains have a significant impact on the law enforcement community, providing essential support and enhancing the overall well-being of officers and their families.

4.5.1 Enhancing Officer Well-Being

Part-time chaplains play a crucial role in enhancing the emotional and spiritual well-being of officers. Their support helps officers manage stress, cope with trauma, and maintain their mental health.

4.5.2 Strengthening Community Ties

By engaging with the community, part-time chaplains help to build positive relationships between law enforcement and the public. Their efforts promote trust, understanding, and collaboration, fostering a stronger, more cohesive community.

4.5.3 Providing Continuity

Part-time chaplains provide continuity in support, offering a consistent presence that officers can rely on during times of need. This continuity helps to build trust and strengthen the chaplain-officer relationship.

4.5.4 Encouraging Resilience

Through their counseling and support, part-time chaplains help officers develop resilience, enabling them to recover more effectively from stress and trauma. This resilience is essential for the long-term well-being and effectiveness of the force.

4.6 Case Studies and Real-Life Examples

Real-life examples illustrate the significant contributions of part-time chaplains to the law enforcement community. These case studies highlight the ways in which part-time chaplains provide essential support and make a positive impact.

4.6.1 Balancing Dual Roles

Chaplain Jessica, a part-time police chaplain and full-time social worker, balances her dual roles effectively. She uses her expertise in social work to provide valuable counseling and support to officers. Despite her busy schedule, she remains committed to being present for critical incidents and providing ongoing support to the department. Her ability to integrate her skills from both roles enhances her effectiveness as a chaplain.

4.6.2 Providing Flexible Support

Officer Tim experienced a personal crisis outside of regular working hours. The part-time chaplain, aware of Tim's situation, made herself available for a late-night counseling session. Her flexibility and willingness to adjust her schedule provided Tim with the immediate support he needed, demonstrating the value of having adaptable part-time chaplains within the force.

4.6.3 Enhancing Community Engagement

Part-time chaplain David, who also serves as a local pastor, leveraged his community connections to organize a joint community-police event. This event included workshops on stress management, community-building activities, and opportunities for officers and community members to interact. David's dual role facilitated a successful event that strengthened community ties and promoted mutual understanding.

4.7 Essential Qualities for Part-Time Chaplains

Part-time chaplains must possess specific qualities and skills to effectively fulfill their role. These qualities include:

4.7.1 Flexibility

Flexibility is essential for managing the varied and unpredictable nature of part-time chaplaincy. Part-time chaplains must be able to adapt to changing circumstances and respond to diverse needs.

4.7.2 Commitment

A strong commitment to the role is crucial for part-time chaplains, given the demands and challenges of balancing multiple responsibilities. This commitment drives their dedication to providing consistent and reliable support.

4.7.3 Time Management

Effective time management is vital for balancing chaplaincy duties with other professional or personal commitments. Part-time chaplains must prioritize tasks and manage their schedules to fulfill their duties effectively.

4.7.4 Professionalism

Professionalism ensures that part-time chaplains uphold high standards of conduct and integrity. This professionalism fosters trust and respect within the law enforcement community.

4.8 Conclusion

Part-time chaplains play a vital role in supporting the law enforcement community, balancing their duties with other professional responsibilities while offering flexibility and adaptability in their service. Their contributions enhance the well-being of officers, strengthen community ties, and provide crucial emotional and spiritual support during times of crisis. Through their dedicated service, part-time chaplains help foster a more resilient and cohesive police force, ultimately contributing to the overall effectiveness and health of law enforcement agencies. Their unique ability to integrate chaplaincy work with other roles brings a diverse perspective and enriches the support system available to officers and their families.

FULL-TIME CHAPLAINS

Full-time chaplains are fully integrated into the police force, providing consistent and comprehensive support across various aspects of law enforcement. Their role is essential in offering continuous spiritual, emotional, and psychological care to officers, their families, and the community. This chapter explores the responsibilities, benefits, challenges, and impact of full-time chaplains within the police force.

4.1 The Role of Full-Time Chaplains

Full-time chaplains perform a wide range of duties, ensuring that they are available to meet the needs of the police force at all times. Their responsibilities include spiritual counseling, crisis intervention, conducting ceremonies, and community engagement. By being fully integrated into the police force, they can provide a consistent and reliable presence, fostering trust and support.

4.1.1 Spiritual Counseling

Full-time chaplains offer ongoing spiritual counseling to officers and their families, helping them navigate personal and professional challenges. This counseling includes:

- Individual Counseling: Providing one-on-one support to address personal concerns, stress, and emotional well-being.

- Group Support Sessions: Facilitating group support sessions for officers to share experiences and offer mutual support.

- Faith-Based Guidance: Offering faith-based advice and support tailored to the individual's beliefs and values.

4.1.2 Crisis Intervention

Full-time chaplains provide immediate and ongoing support during crises, including:

- On-Scene Response: Responding to critical incidents to offer comfort and reassurance.

- Follow-Up Care: Providing ongoing counseling and support after a crisis to help individuals process their experiences.

- Resource Connection: Connecting officers and their families with additional resources, such as mental health professionals and support groups.

4.1.3 Conducting Ceremonies

Full-time chaplains officiate various ceremonies, including:

- Weddings: Conducting wedding ceremonies for officers and their families.

- Funerals and Memorial Services: Leading funeral and memorial services to honor fallen officers and provide comfort to grieving families.

- Departmental Events: Participating in promotions, retirements, and other ceremonial events within the department.

4.1.4 Community Engagement

Full-time chaplains engage with the broader community to foster positive relationships between law enforcement and the public. This includes:

- Public Outreach: Participating in community events and activities to build trust and understanding.

- Educational Programs: Leading workshops and seminars on topics such as stress management, ethics, and resilience.

- Interfaith Collaboration: Working with religious and community leaders to promote inclusivity and support within the community.

4.2 Benefits of Full-Time Chaplains

Full-time chaplains offer several benefits to the law enforcement community due to their continuous presence and comprehensive support.

4.2.1 Consistent Support

Full-time chaplains provide consistent support, ensuring that officers and their families have access to reliable spiritual and emotional care whenever needed. This consistency helps build trust and strengthen relationships within the force.

4.2.2 Immediate Availability

Being fully integrated into the police force allows full-time chaplains to be immediately available during crises and critical incidents. Their presence can provide immediate comfort and stability during challenging times.

4.2.3 Deep Integration

Full-time chaplains become deeply integrated into the culture and dynamics of the police force. This integration enables them to understand the unique challenges and needs of officers, enhancing the effectiveness of their support.

4.2.4 Comprehensive Care

Full-time chaplains can offer comprehensive care, addressing the spiritual, emotional, and psychological needs of officers and their families. Their continuous presence allows them to provide ongoing support and follow-up care.

4.3 Challenges Faced by Full-Time Chaplains

Despite the benefits, full-time chaplains face unique challenges in their role. Understanding these challenges is essential for appreciating their dedication and resilience.

4.3.1 Emotional Toll

The emotional demands of providing continuous support during crises and critical incidents can take a toll on full-time chaplains. They must develop strategies for self-care and resilience to manage the emotional impact of their work.

4.3.2 High Expectations

Full-time chaplains may face high expectations from officers, families, and the department to be available at all times. Balancing these expectations with personal well-being can be challenging.

4.3.3 Burnout Risk

The risk of burnout is higher for full-time chaplains due to the continuous and intensive nature of their work. They must find ways to maintain their well-being and prevent burnout while fulfilling their duties.

4.3.4 Maintaining Boundaries

Maintaining professional boundaries while being fully integrated into the police force can be complex. Full-time chaplains must navigate the potential overlap between their personal and professional lives.

4.4 Strategies for Effective Service

Full-time chaplains use various strategies to manage their responsibilities effectively and provide meaningful support to the law enforcement community.

4.4.1 Self-Care Practices

Engaging in self-care practices is crucial for full-time chaplains to maintain their well-being. This includes regular exercise, adequate rest, and engaging in activities that promote mental and emotional health.

4.4.2 Continuous Professional Development

Continuous professional development is essential for staying current with best practices and enhancing skills. Full-time chaplains must attend training sessions, workshops, and conferences to improve their effectiveness.

4.4.3 Building a Support Network

Building a support network within the department and among fellow chaplains can provide additional resources and emotional support. Collaboration with colleagues can enhance the chaplain's ability to meet the needs of the force.

4.4.4 Time Management

Effective time management is vital for balancing the demands of full-time chaplaincy. Full-time chaplains must prioritize tasks and manage their schedules to fulfill their duties effectively.

4.5 The Impact of Full-Time Chaplains

Full-time chaplains have a significant impact on the law enforcement community, providing essential support and enhancing the overall well-being of officers and their families.

4.5.1 Enhancing Officer Well-Being

Full-time chaplains play a crucial role in enhancing the emotional and spiritual well-being of officers. Their support helps officers manage stress, cope with trauma, and maintain their mental health.

4.5.2 Strengthening Community Ties

By engaging with the community, full-time chaplains help to build positive relationships between law enforcement and the public. Their efforts promote trust, understanding, and collaboration, fostering a stronger, more cohesive community.

4.5.3 Providing Continuity

Full-time chaplains provide continuity in support, offering a consistent presence that officers can rely on during times of need. This continuity helps to build trust and strengthen the chaplain-officer relationship.

4.5.4 Encouraging Resilience

Through their counseling and support, full-time chaplains help officers develop resilience, enabling them to recover more effectively from stress and trauma. This resilience is essential for the long-term well-being and effectiveness of the force.

4.6 Case Studies and Real-Life Examples

Real-life examples illustrate the significant contributions of full-time chaplains to the law enforcement community. These case studies highlight the ways in which full-time chaplains provide essential support and make a positive impact.

4.6.1 Continuous Support During a Crisis

Following a major natural disaster, the full-time chaplain was on the scene to provide immediate emotional and spiritual support to the affected officers and their families.

The chaplain's continuous presence throughout the recovery period provided stability and reassurance, helping the community to heal and rebuild.

4.6.2 Building Trust Through Daily Interaction

Chaplain Mark, a full-time police chaplain, made a point to attend roll calls, departmental meetings, and training sessions regularly. His consistent presence and engagement with officers built trust and rapport, making him a trusted confidant and advisor for many officers. When critical incidents occurred, officers felt comfortable seeking his support due to the strong relationships he had built.

4.6.3 Comprehensive Care for an Officer's Family

When Officer Lisa was diagnosed with a serious illness, the full-time chaplain provided continuous support to her and her family. The chaplain offered spiritual counseling, coordinated practical assistance, and connected the family with additional resources. This comprehensive care helped Lisa and her family navigate the challenges of her illness with strength and resilience.

4.7 Essential Qualities for Full-Time Chaplains

Full-time chaplains must possess specific qualities and skills to effectively fulfill their role. These qualities include:

4.7.1 Compassion

Compassion is essential for understanding and addressing the emotional needs of officers and their families. Full-time chaplains must demonstrate genuine care and concern for those they serve.

4.7.2 Commitment

A strong commitment to the role is crucial for full-time chaplains, given the demands and challenges of their work. This commitment drives their dedication to providing consistent and reliable support.

4.7.3 Resilience

Resilience is important for managing the emotional toll of continuous support during crises and critical incidents. Full-time chaplains must develop strategies for maintaining their well-being and preventing burnout.

4.7.4 Professionalism

Professionalism ensures that full-time chaplains uphold high standards of conduct and integrity. This professionalism fosters trust and respect within the law enforcement community.

4.8 Conclusion

Full-time chaplains play a vital role in supporting the law enforcement community, providing consistent and comprehensive support across various aspects of law enforcement. Their continuous presence enhances the well-being of officers, strengthens community ties, and promotes resilience. Despite the challenges they face, full-time chaplains demonstrate remarkable dedication and commitment, making a profound impact on the police force and the broader community.

This chapter has explored the unique contributions, benefits, challenges, and impact of full-time chaplains. Subsequent chapters will delve deeper into other roles and responsibilities of police chaplains, including specialized chaplains and the unique challenges and rewards of this essential vocation.

SPECIALIZED CHAPLAINS

Some chaplains specialize in specific areas, such as SWAT teams or crisis negotiation units, bringing targeted expertise to these high-stakes roles. Specialized chaplains provide focused support tailored to the unique challenges and demands of their assigned units. This chapter explores the roles, responsibilities, benefits, challenges, and impact of specialized chaplains within the law enforcement community.

4.1 The Role of Specialized Chaplains

Specialized chaplains perform duties tailored to the specific needs of the units they serve. These chaplains undergo additional training and develop expertise in particular areas to provide effective support. Their roles include spiritual counseling, crisis intervention, training and support during operations, and conducting specialized ceremonies.

4.1.1 Spiritual Counseling

Specialized chaplains offer spiritual counseling to members of their assigned units, helping them navigate personal and professional challenges. This counseling includes:

- Individual Support: Providing one-on-one counseling to address specific concerns and stressors related to their specialized roles.

- Group Sessions: Facilitating group support sessions to foster camaraderie and mutual support among team members.

- Faith-Based Guidance: Offering faith-based advice and support tailored to the unique challenges of specialized units.

4.1.2 Crisis Intervention

Specialized chaplains provide immediate and ongoing support during crises, including:

- On-Scene Response: Responding to critical incidents involving their specialized units, such as SWAT operations or hostage situations.

- Follow-Up Care: Providing ongoing counseling and support after a crisis to help team members process their experiences.

- Resource Connection: Connecting team members with additional resources, such as mental health professionals and specialized support groups.

4.1.3 Training and Support

Specialized chaplains participate in training and provide support during operations, including:

- Pre-Operation Briefings: Offering spiritual support and guidance before high-stakes operations.

- On-Site Presence: Being present during operations to provide immediate emotional and spiritual support.

- Post-Operation Debriefings: Conducting debriefings and providing counseling to help team members process their experiences and maintain mental health.

4.1.4 Conducting Specialized Ceremonies

Specialized chaplains officiate ceremonies tailored to their units, including:

- Promotion and Award Ceremonies: Recognizing achievements and milestones within the specialized units.

- Memorial Services: Honoring fallen team members and providing comfort to their families and colleagues.

- Team-Building Events: Leading ceremonies and activities designed to strengthen bonds and foster a sense of unity within the team.

4.2 Benefits of Specialized Chaplains

Specialized chaplains offer several benefits to their units due to their targeted expertise and focused support.

4.2.1 Targeted Expertise

Specialized chaplains bring targeted expertise to their roles, allowing them to address the specific challenges and needs of their units effectively. Their specialized knowledge enhances the support they provide.

4.2.2 Enhanced Trust

Being embedded within specialized units allows chaplains to build strong relationships and trust with team members. This trust is crucial for providing effective emotional and spiritual support.

4.2.3 Immediate Support

Specialized chaplains are often present during high-stakes operations, providing immediate support when it is needed most. Their presence can help stabilize situations and offer reassurance to team members.

4.2.4 Comprehensive Care

Specialized chaplains offer comprehensive care tailored to the unique demands of their units. This care includes ongoing support, crisis intervention, and specialized training, contributing to the overall well-being of team members.

4.3 Challenges Faced by Specialized Chaplains

Despite the benefits, specialized chaplains face unique challenges in their roles. Understanding these challenges is essential for appreciating their dedication and resilience.

4.3.1 High-Stress Environments

Specialized chaplains often work in high-stress environments, such as during SWAT operations or crisis negotiations. Managing their own stress while providing support to team members can be challenging.

4.3.2 Emotional Toll

The emotional demands of supporting team members through high-stakes situations can take a toll on specialized chaplains. They must develop strategies for self-care and resilience to manage the emotional impact of their work.

4.3.3 Intensive Training

Specialized chaplains require intensive training to understand the specific needs and challenges of their units. This training can be demanding and time-consuming.

4.3.4 Maintaining Boundaries

Maintaining professional boundaries while being deeply embedded within specialized units can be complex.

Specialized chaplains must navigate the potential overlap between their personal and professional lives.

4.4 Strategies for Effective Service

Specialized chaplains use various strategies to manage their responsibilities effectively and provide meaningful support to their units.

4.4.1 Specialized Training

Engaging in specialized training is crucial for understanding the unique needs and challenges of their units. This training includes:

- SWAT Team Training: Understanding the operational dynamics and stressors of SWAT teams.

- Crisis Negotiation Training: Learning techniques for supporting negotiators during high-stakes situations.

- Tactical Operations Training: Gaining insights into the procedures and challenges of tactical operations.

4.4.2 Building Strong Relationships

Building strong relationships with team members is essential for effective support. Specialized chaplains must:

- Engage Regularly: Participate in regular team activities and training sessions.

- Show Commitment: Demonstrate a genuine commitment to the well-being of team members.

- Foster Trust: Create an environment of trust and mutual respect.

4.4.3 Self-Care Practices

Engaging in self-care practices is crucial for maintaining their well-being. Specialized chaplains must:

- Manage Stress: Practice stress management techniques, such as mindfulness and relaxation exercises.

- Seek Support: Access peer support and counseling to process their own experiences.

- Maintain Balance: Balance their professional responsibilities with personal well-being.

4.4.4 Continuous Professional Development

Continuous professional development is essential for staying current with best practices and enhancing skills. Specialized chaplains must:

- Attend Training Sessions: Participate in ongoing training and professional development opportunities.

- Stay Informed: Keep up-to-date with the latest research and developments in their field.

- Enhance Skills: Continuously work on enhancing their counseling and support skills.

4.5 The Impact of Specialized Chaplains

Specialized chaplains have a significant impact on their units, providing essential support and enhancing the overall well-being of team members.

4.5.1 Enhancing Team Well-Being

Specialized chaplains play a crucial role in enhancing the emotional and spiritual well-being of team members. Their support helps team members manage stress, cope with trauma, and maintain their mental health.

4.5.2 Improving Operational Effectiveness

By providing targeted support, specialized chaplains contribute to the overall effectiveness of their units. Their presence can help stabilize situations and enhance team cohesion and morale.

4.5.3 Strengthening Trust and Cohesion

Specialized chaplains help to build trust and cohesion within their units. Their ongoing presence and support foster a sense of unity and mutual respect among team members.

4.5.4 Promoting Resilience

Through their counseling and support, specialized chaplains help team members develop resilience, enabling them to recover more effectively from stress and trauma. This resilience is essential for the long-term well-being and effectiveness of the units.

4.6 Case Studies and Real-Life Examples

Real-life examples illustrate the significant contributions of specialized chaplains to their units. These case studies highlight the ways in which specialized chaplains provide essential support and make a positive impact.

4.6.1 Supporting a SWAT Team During a High-Risk Operation

During a high-risk operation, the specialized chaplain was embedded with the SWAT team, providing immediate spiritual and emotional support. The chaplain's presence helped to calm the team members and offered a sense of reassurance. After the operation, the chaplain conducted debriefing sessions to help team members process their experiences and maintain their mental health.

4.6.2 Providing Crisis Negotiation Support

In a hostage situation, the specialized chaplain provided support to the crisis negotiation unit. The chaplain offered spiritual guidance and emotional support to the negotiators, helping them manage the stress and pressure of the situation. The chaplain's support contributed to the successful resolution of the crisis and the well-being of the negotiation team.

4.6.3 Enhancing Team Cohesion

Chaplain Laura, a specialized chaplain for a tactical unit, organized regular team-building activities and ceremonies. These events helped to strengthen the bonds among team members and fostered a sense of unity and trust. Laura's efforts contributed to improved team cohesion and morale, enhancing the overall effectiveness of the unit.

4.7 Essential Qualities for Specialized Chaplains

Specialized chaplains must possess specific qualities and skills to effectively fulfill their role. These qualities include:

4.7.1 Expertise

Expertise in the specific area of specialization is essential for understanding the unique challenges and needs of the units. Specialized chaplains must continually enhance their knowledge and skills.

4.7.2 Resilience

Resilience is important for managing the emotional toll of supporting team members through high-stakes situations. Specialized chaplains must develop strategies for maintaining their well-being and preventing burnout.

4.7.3 Flexibility

Flexibility is crucial for adapting to the dynamic and unpredictable nature of specialized units. Specialized chaplains must be able to respond to changing circumstances and diverse needs.

4.7.4 Professionalism

Professionalism ensures that specialized chaplains uphold high standards of conduct and integrity. This professionalism fosters trust and respect within their units.

4.8 Conclusion

Specialized chaplains play a vital role in supporting specific units within the law enforcement community, bringing targeted expertise and focused support to high-stakes roles. Their contributions enhance the well-being of team members, improve operational effectiveness, and promote resilience. Despite the challenges they face, specialized chaplains demonstrate remarkable dedication and commitment, making a profound impact on their units and the broader community.

CHAPTER 05

DAILY LIFE OF A POLICE CHAPLAIN

A Typical Day

The daily life of a police chaplain is diverse and dynamic, filled with various responsibilities that require adaptability, compassion, and resilience. This chapter provides an overview of a typical day in the life of a police chaplain, illustrating the breadth of their duties and the significant impact they have on the law enforcement community.

5.1 Morning Routine

5.1.1 Starting the Day with Reflection

Many police chaplains begin their day with a period of personal reflection or prayer. This practice helps center them spiritually and mentally, preparing them for the demands of the day ahead.

5.1.2 Checking Communications

After reflection, chaplains typically check their emails, messages, and any urgent communications from the police department. Staying informed about ongoing situations and upcoming events is crucial for effective support.

5.2 Morning Briefings and Roll Calls

5.2.1 Attending Roll Calls

Police chaplains often attend morning roll calls or briefings with officers. This presence allows them to stay connected with the team, understand the day's assignments, and offer a brief word of encouragement or a prayer.

5.2.2 Providing Support

During roll calls, chaplains may identify officers who seem stressed or troubled and offer immediate support or schedule follow-up conversations. Their availability and visibility during these times foster trust and accessibility.

5.3 Counseling and Support Sessions

5.3.1 Individual Counseling

A significant part of a chaplain's day is spent providing individual counseling sessions. These sessions can address various issues, such as:

- Personal Challenges: Helping officers deal with personal issues like marital problems, grief, or financial stress.

- Professional Stress: Assisting officers in managing job-related stress, ethical dilemmas, and trauma from critical incidents.

5.3.2 Group Support Meetings

Chaplains may also facilitate group support meetings, providing a space for officers to share experiences, offer mutual support, and discuss coping strategies. These meetings can be formal, like scheduled support groups, or informal gatherings.

5.4 Crisis ntervention

5.4.1 Responding to Emergencies

When critical incidents occur, chaplains must be ready to respond immediately. This can involve:

- On-Scene Support: Providing emotional and spiritual support at the scene of an accident, crime, or other traumatic event.

- Hospital Visits: Visiting injured officers or victims in the hospital to offer comfort and support to them and their families.

5.4.2 Follow-Up Care

After an initial crisis, chaplains provide follow-up care to ensure ongoing support for affected individuals. This can include regular check-ins, additional counseling sessions, and connecting officers with further resources.

5.5 Administrative Duties

5.5.1 Documentation

Chaplains have administrative responsibilities, including documenting their interactions and the support provided. This helps in tracking the needs of officers and ensuring continuity of care.

5.5.2 Planning and Coordination

Chaplains spend part of their day planning events, coordinating with other support services, and preparing for upcoming ceremonies or community outreach activities.

5.6 Community Engagement

5.6.1 Public Outreach

Engaging with the community is a vital part of a chaplain's role. This can involve:

- Attending Community Events: Participating in local events to build bridges between the police and the community.

- Educational Programs: Leading workshops on topics such as stress management, ethics, and resilience.

5.6.2 Interfaith Collaboration

Chaplains often work with local religious leaders and organizations to promote interfaith understanding and support within the community. This collaboration can enhance the chaplain's ability to provide inclusive and respectful support.

5.7 Conducting Ceremonies

5.7.1 Planning Ceremonies

Chaplains spend part of their day planning and preparing for various ceremonies, such as weddings, funerals, and memorial services. This preparation includes meeting with families, selecting readings, and coordinating logistics.

5.7.2 Officiating Events

Chaplains officiate ceremonies, providing spiritual and emotional support during significant life events. Their presence helps bring comfort and a sense of continuity to officers and their families.

5.8 Evening Routine

5.8.1 Reflecting on the Day

At the end of the day, chaplains often spend time reflecting on their interactions and the support they provided. This reflection helps them process their experiences and plan for the following day.

5.8.2 Self-Care

Engaging in self-care is crucial for chaplains to maintain their well-being. Evening routines may include activities such as exercise, spending time with family, reading, or pursuing hobbies.

5.9 Case Studies and Real-Life Examples

Real-life examples illustrate the diverse and dynamic nature of a police chaplain's daily life. These case studies highlight the significant impact chaplains have on the law enforcement community.

5.9.1 Responding to a Critical Incident

One evening, Chaplain Sarah received a call about a critical incident involving a shooting. She immediately went to the scene, providing comfort to the officers involved and offering prayers for the victims. Afterward, she visited the hospital to support the injured officer's family and coordinated follow-up care to ensure they received ongoing support.

5.9.2 Conducting a Memorial Service

Chaplain John spent the morning preparing for a memorial service for a fallen officer. He met with the officer's family to discuss their wishes, selected meaningful readings, and coordinated with the department. During the service, his words of comfort and the ceremony he conducted provided solace to the grieving family and colleagues.

5.9.3 Facilitating a Stress Management Workshop

In the afternoon, Chaplain Maria led a stress management workshop for officers. She provided practical techniques for managing stress, facilitated group discussions, and offered individual support to those who needed it. The workshop helped officers develop resilience and improved their overall well-being.

5.10 Essential Qualities for Police Chaplains

The diverse and dynamic nature of a police chaplain's work requires specific qualities and skills, including:

5.10.1 Compassion

Compassion is essential for understanding and addressing the emotional needs of officers and their families. Chaplains must demonstrate genuine care and concern for those they serve.

5.10.2 Flexibility

Flexibility is crucial for adapting to the varied and unpredictable nature of their work. Chaplains must be able to respond to emergencies, manage multiple responsibilities, and adjust their plans as needed.

5.10.3 Resilience

Resilience is important for managing the emotional toll of their work. Chaplains must develop strategies for maintaining their well-being and preventing burnout.

5.10.4 Communication Skills

Effective communication skills are vital for providing support, offering guidance, and leading ceremonies. Chaplains must be able to articulate their thoughts and emotions clearly and empathetically.

5.11 Conclusion

The daily life of a police chaplain is diverse and dynamic, filled with various responsibilities that require adaptability, compassion, and resilience. From providing spiritual counseling and crisis intervention to conducting ceremonies and engaging with the community, chaplains play a vital role in supporting the law enforcement community. Their work has a profound impact on the well-being of officers, their families, and the broader community.

This chapter has provided an overview of a typical day in the life of a police chaplain, illustrating the breadth of their duties and the significant impact they have. Subsequent chapters will delve deeper into other aspects of police chaplaincy, including the challenges and rewards of this essential vocation.

BALANCING ADMINISTRATIVE DUTIES AND FILED WORK

Introduction

Effective police chaplaincy requires balancing administrative responsibilities with hands-on support in the field. This balance is crucial for providing comprehensive care to law enforcement officers and their families. This chapter explores how chaplains manage these dual roles, the challenges they face, and the strategies they use to maintain efficiency and effectiveness in their service.

5.1 Understanding Administrative Duties

Administrative duties are a significant part of a police chaplain's role, encompassing a variety of tasks that support the overall functioning of the chaplaincy program. These duties include documentation, planning, coordination, and communication.

5.1.1 Documentation

Proper documentation is essential for tracking interactions, support provided, and the needs of officers and their families. This includes:

- Counseling Records: Keeping detailed records of counseling sessions while maintaining confidentiality.

- Incident Reports: Documenting support provided during critical incidents.

- Activity Logs: Recording participation in events, training sessions, and community outreach activities.

5.1.2 Planning and Coordination

Chaplains are involved in planning and coordinating various activities and programs. This includes:

- Ceremonies and Events: Organizing and preparing for weddings, funerals, memorial services, and departmental events.

- Support Programs: Developing and managing support programs, such as peer support groups and stress management workshops.

- Training Sessions: Coordinating training for officers on topics like ethics, resilience, and mental health.

5.1.3 Communication

Effective communication is vital for coordinating with officers, department leaders, and community members. This includes:

- Regular Updates: Providing regular updates to department leadership on chaplaincy activities and officer well-being.

- Networking: Building relationships with other chaplains, religious leaders, and community organizations.

- Resource Referral: Communicating with external support services to refer officers and their families for additional assistance.

5.2 Field Work Responsibilities

Field work is a core aspect of a police chaplain's role, involving direct interaction with officers and their families, crisis intervention, and community engagement.

5.2.1 Direct Interaction

Building relationships through direct interaction is crucial for providing effective support. This includes:

- Regular Presence: Being visible and accessible to officers, attending roll calls, and participating in departmental activities.

- One-on-One Support: Offering individual counseling and support tailored to the specific needs of officers.

- Group Support: Facilitating group support sessions and peer support programs.

5.2.2 Crisis Intervention

Responding to crises is a critical component of field work. This includes:

- On-Scene Response: Providing immediate support at the scene of accidents, crimes, and other traumatic events.

- Hospital Visits: Visiting injured officers or victims in the hospital to offer comfort and support.

- Follow-Up Care: Ensuring ongoing support and counseling after critical incidents.

5.2.3 Community Engagement

Engaging with the community helps build trust and positive relationships between law enforcement and the public. This includes:

- Public Outreach: Participating in community events, educational programs, and outreach activities.

- Interfaith Collaboration: Working with religious leaders and community organizations to promote inclusivity and support.

- Workshops and Seminars: Leading educational sessions on topics relevant to both officers and the community.

5.3 Challenges in Balancing Administrative and Field Work

Balancing administrative duties with field work presents several challenges. Understanding these challenges is essential for developing effective strategies to manage them.

5.3.1 Time Management

Managing time effectively is one of the biggest challenges, as chaplains must juggle various responsibilities. This includes:

- Prioritizing Tasks: Identifying and focusing on the most critical tasks.

- Scheduling: Allocating specific times for administrative work and field duties.

- Flexibility: Being adaptable to changes and urgent needs that arise.

5.3.2 Emotional Toll

The emotional demands of crisis intervention and providing support can impact a chaplain's ability to manage administrative tasks. Strategies for addressing this include:

- Self-Care: Practicing self-care and seeking support when needed.

- Delegation: Delegating administrative tasks when possible to balance the workload.

- Boundaries: Setting boundaries to ensure adequate time for rest and recovery.

5.3.3 Maintaining Focus

Switching between administrative duties and fieldwork can be challenging and may impact focus and efficiency. Strategies to maintain focus include:

- Task Segmentation: Dividing the day into dedicated time blocks for administrative tasks and fieldwork.

- Minimizing Distractions: Creating a focused work environment for administrative duties.

- Mindfulness Practices: Using mindfulness techniques to stay present and engaged in each task.

5.4 Strategies for Effective Balance

Chaplains employ various strategies to balance their administrative and field work responsibilities effectively. These strategies help ensure that they can provide comprehensive and efficient support to the law enforcement community.

5.4.1 Structured Scheduling

Creating a structured schedule helps manage time effectively and ensures that both administrative and fieldwork responsibilities are addressed. This includes:

- Daily Planning: Develop a daily plan that outlines specific times for administrative tasks and field duties.

- Flexibility: Allowing for flexibility to accommodate urgent needs and unexpected events.

- Regular Review: Reviewing and adjusting the schedule regularly to ensure it remains effective.

5.4.2 Delegation and Teamwork

Delegating tasks and working as part of a team can help balance the workload and ensure that all responsibilities are met. This includes:

- Collaborating with Staff: Working with administrative staff to handle paperwork and coordination tasks.

- Leveraging Volunteers: Utilizing volunteers to assist with community outreach and support programs.

- Team Approach: Collaborating with other chaplains and support personnel to share responsibilities and provide comprehensive care.

5.4.3 Technology and Tools

Using technology and tools can enhance efficiency and streamline administrative tasks. This includes:

- Digital Documentation: Using digital tools for record-keeping and documentation to save time and improve accuracy.

- Communication Platforms: Utilizing communication platforms for efficient coordination and information sharing.

- Scheduling Tools: Implementing scheduling tools to manage appointments, meetings, and events effectively.

5.4.4 Continuous Improvement

Continuously improving processes and strategies helps maintain balance and enhance effectiveness. This includes:

- Training and Development: Participating in training and professional development to improve skills and knowledge.

- Feedback and Evaluation: Seeking feedback from officers and colleagues to identify areas for improvement.

- Adaptability: Being open to new approaches and strategies to improve efficiency and effectiveness.

5.5 The Impact of Balanced Chaplaincy

Maintaining a balance between administrative duties and field work has a significant impact on the effectiveness of police chaplaincy and the well-being of officers and their families.

5.5.1 Comprehensive Support

Balancing administrative and field work ensures that chaplains can provide comprehensive support, addressing both the organizational needs of the chaplaincy program and the personal needs of officers.

5.5.2 Enhanced Efficiency

Effective time management and delegation enhance efficiency, allowing chaplains to accomplish more and provide timely support.

5.5.3 Improved Officer Well-Being

By managing their responsibilities effectively, chaplains can offer consistent and reliable support, contributing to the overall well-being and resilience of officers and their families.

5.5.4 Positive Community Relationships

Balanced chaplaincy fosters positive relationships between law enforcement and the community, promoting trust, understanding, and collaboration.

5.6 Case Studies and Real-Life Examples

Real-life examples illustrate how chaplains balance their administrative duties and field work, highlighting the strategies they use and the impact of their efforts.

5.6.1 Structured Scheduling for Crisis Intervention

Chaplain Emily uses a structured schedule to balance her responsibilities. She dedicates mornings to administrative tasks, ensuring that documentation and planning are completed efficiently. Afternoons are reserved for field work, allowing her to provide direct support and respond to emergencies. This structured approach enables Emily to manage her workload effectively and provide comprehensive care.

5.6.2 Delegation and Team Collaboration

Chaplain Mike collaborates closely with administrative staff and volunteers to handle paperwork and coordination tasks. By delegating these responsibilities, Mike can focus on providing direct support to officers and their families. This teamwork approach enhances efficiency and ensures that all aspects of the chaplaincy program are well-managed.

5.6.3 Utilizing Technology for Efficiency

Chaplain Sarah lverages technology to streamline her administrative tasks. She uses digital tools for documentation, communication platforms for coordination, and scheduling tools to manage her appointments and events. This use of technology saves time and improves accuracy, allowing Sarah to dedicate more time to fieldwork and direct support.

5.7 Essential Qualities for Balancing Roles

Balancing administrative duties and field work requires specific qualities and skills, including:

5.7.1 Organization

Strong organizational skills are essential for managing multiple responsibilities effectively. Chaplains must be able to prioritize tasks, manage their time, and maintain focus.

5.7.2 Adaptability

Adaptability is crucial for responding to changing circumstances and urgent needs. Chaplains must be flexible and open to adjusting their plans as needed.

5.7.3 Resilience

Resilience is important for managing the emotional toll of their work. Chaplains must develop strategies for maintaining their well-being and preventing burnout.

5.7.4 Communication Skills

Effective communication skills are vital for coordinating with officers, department leaders, and community members. Chaplains must be able to articulate their thoughts and emotions clearly and empathetically.

5.8 Conclusion

Balancing administrative duties and fieldwork is essential for effective police chaplaincy. By managing these dual roles effectively, chaplains can provide comprehensive care to law enforcement officers and their families. Through structured scheduling, delegation, use of technology, and continuous improvement, chaplains enhance their efficiency and effectiveness, contributing to the overall well-being of the law enforcement community.

HANDLING EMERGENCIES AND CRITICAL INCIDENTS

Introduction

Police chaplains are often on the front lines during emergencies, providing immediate and long-term support to those affected by critical incidents. Their presence and intervention can be crucial in stabilizing situations, offering comfort, and facilitating recovery. This chapter explores the role of police chaplains in handling emergencies and critical incidents, the strategies they employ, the challenges they face, and the impact of their work.

5.1 Understanding Emergencies and Critical Incidents

Emergencies and critical incidents in law enforcement can range from natural disasters and accidents to violent crimes and officer-involved shootings. These events can cause significant emotional and psychological distress to officers, victims, and their families. Police chaplains play a vital role in addressing these impacts through their immediate response and ongoing support.

5.1.1 Types of Critical Incidents

Critical incidents that police chaplains respond to include:

- Officer-Involved Shootings: Incidents where officers are involved in shootings, resulting in injury or death.

- Line-of-Duty Deaths: Deaths of officers while performing their duties.

- Natural Disasters: Events such as hurricanes, floods, and earthquakes affecting the community and law enforcement personnel.

- Accidents: Serious accidents involving officers or members of the public.

- Violent Crimes: Homicides, assaults, and other violent crimes impacting officers and the community.

5.2 Immediate Response

The immediate response of police chaplains during emergencies is crucial for providing emotional and spiritual support, stabilizing the situation, and ensuring the well-being of those affected.

5.2.1 On-Scene Presence

Chaplains often arrive at the scene of critical incidents to provide immediate support. Their presence helps to:

- Calm and Reassure: Offering words of comfort and reassurance to officers and victims.

- Provide Emotional Support: Helping individuals manage shock, fear, and grief.

- Assist with Practical Needs: Addressing immediate practical needs, such as contacting family members or providing information about the next steps.

5.2.2 Hospital Visits

When officers or victims are injured and taken to the hospital, chaplains visit to offer support. This includes:

- Supporting Families: Providing comfort and information to the families of injured officers or victims.

- Praying or Offering Spiritual Support: Conducting prayers or other spiritual practices based on the individual's beliefs.

- Coordinating with Medical Staff: Working with medical staff to ensure the needs of the injured and their families are met.

5.3 Long-Term Support

Beyond the immediate response, police chaplains provide ongoing support to help individuals cope with the aftermath of critical incidents and facilitate long-term recovery.

5.3.1 Follow-Up Counseling

Chaplains offer follow-up counseling to officers, victims, and their families, addressing the emotional and psychological impacts of the incident. This includes:

- One-on-One Counseling: Providing individual support to help process trauma and grief.

- Group Support Sessions: Facilitating group discussions and peer support to foster a sense of community and shared understanding.

- Referral to Additional Resources: Connecting individuals with mental health professionals, support groups, and other resources.

5.3.2 Memorial Services and Ceremonies

Chaplains organize and conduct memorial services and ceremonies to honor those who have been affected by critical incidents. These services provide a space for:

- Grieving and Remembrance: Allowing officers and the community to grieve and remember those lost.

- Celebrating Lives: Celebrating the lives and contributions of fallen officers.

- Providing Closure: Helping individuals find closure and begin the healing process.

5.4 Strategies for Effective Intervention

Effective intervention by police chaplains during emergencies and critical incidents requires specific strategies and skills. These strategies help chaplains provide meaningful support and address the diverse needs of those affected.

5.4.1 Training and Preparation

Chaplains must be well-trained and prepared to handle critical incidents. This includes:

- Crisis Intervention Training: Learning techniques for managing emotional and psychological distress.

- Scenario-Based Training: Participating in scenario-based training exercises to simulate real-life emergencies.

- Continuous Professional Development: Engaging in ongoing training and education to stay current with best practices.

5.4.2 Building Trust and Rapport

Building trust and rapport with officers and the community is essential for effective intervention. This involves:

- Regular Interaction: Maintaining a visible and approachable presence within the department.

- Demonstrating Empathy: Showing genuine care and concern for the well-being of others.

- Maintaining Confidentiality: Ensuring that conversations and counseling sessions remain confidential to build trust.

5.4.3 Self-Care and Resilience

Chaplains must practice self-care and build resilience to manage the emotional toll of their work. This includes:

- Seeking Support: Accessing peer support and counseling to process their own experiences.

- Practicing Self-Care: Engaging in activities that promote physical, emotional, and spiritual well-being.

- Setting Boundaries: Establishing boundaries to balance professional responsibilities with personal well-being.

5.5 Challenges Faced by Police Chaplains

Handling emergencies and critical incidents presents several challenges for police chaplains. Understanding these challenges is essential for developing effective strategies to manage them.

5.5.1 Emotional Toll

The emotional demands of supporting individuals through trauma and grief can be overwhelming. Chaplains must find ways to manage their own emotions and prevent burnout.

5.5.2 High-Stress Environments

Working in high-stress environments, such as crime scenes and hospitals, requires chaplains to remain calm and focused while providing support.

5.5.3 Balancing Immediate and Long-Term Support

Chaplains must balance the need for immediate intervention with providing ongoing support. This requires effective time management and prioritization of tasks.

5.5.4 Maintaining Professional Boundaries

Maintaining professional boundaries while building close relationships with officers and their families can be challenging. Chaplains must navigate these boundaries to provide effective support without overstepping.

5.6 Case Studies and Real-Life Examples

Real-life examples illustrate the critical role of police chaplains during emergencies and critical incidents, highlighting their strategies and the impact of their support.

5.6.1 Supporting an Officer-Involved Shooting

Following an officer-involved shooting, Chaplain Tom arrived at the scene to provide immediate support to the involved officers. He offered words of comfort, helped manage the scene's emotional intensity, and coordinated with medical personnel. In the weeks that followed, Chaplain Tom provided ongoing counseling to the officers and their families, helping them process the trauma and begin healing.

5.6.2 Responding to a Natural Disaster

During a major flood, Chaplain Lisa was deployed to assist affected officers and community members. She provided on-scene support, helping to organize relief efforts and offer emotional comfort. Chaplain Lisa also conducted follow-up visits to ensure that those impacted received the necessary support and resources to recover.

5.6.3 Conducting a Memorial Service

After a line-of-duty death, Chaplain John organized a memorial service to honor the fallen officer. He worked closely with the officer's family to plan the service, ensuring it reflected their wishes and provided a meaningful tribute. The service helped the family and colleagues grieve, remember, and find closure.

5.7 Essential Qualities for Handling Emergencies

Handling emergencies and critical incidents requires specific qualities and skills, including:

5.7.1 Compassion

Compassion is essential for understanding and addressing the emotional needs of those affected by critical incidents. Chaplains must demonstrate genuine care and empathy.

5.7.2 Calmness Under Pressure

Remaining calm and composed in high-stress situations is crucial for providing effective support. Chaplains must be able to manage their emotions and stay focused.

5.7.3 Resilience

Resilience is important for coping with the emotional toll of their work. Chaplains must develop strategies for maintaining their well-being and preventing burnout.

5.7.4 Effective Communication

Effective communication skills are vital for providing support, offering guidance, and coordinating with other responders. Chaplains must be able to articulate their thoughts and emotions clearly and empathetically.

5.8 Conclusion

Police chaplains play a vital role in handling emergencies and critical incidents, providing immediate and long-term support to those affected. Their presence and intervention are crucial for stabilizing situations, offering comfort, and facilitating recovery. By employing effective strategies, building trust, and practicing self-care, chaplains can provide meaningful support and address the diverse needs of the law enforcement community.

CHAPTER 06

SERVING THE OFFICERS

Emotional and Mental Health Support

Police chaplains play a crucial role in supporting the mental and emotional well-being of officers, helping them cope with the stresses and traumas of their work. This chapter explores the various ways chaplains provide this support, the strategies they use to address mental health challenges, and the impact of their work on the overall well-being of law enforcement officers.

6.1 Understanding the Stresses and Traumas of Police Work

Law enforcement officers face unique stresses and traumas due to the nature of their work. These can include exposure to violence, dealing with high-pressure situations, and the constant risk to their safety. Understanding these challenges is essential for providing effective support.

6.1.1 Exposure to Violence and Trauma

Officers frequently encounter violent crimes, accidents, and other traumatic events, which can lead to:

- Post-Traumatic Stress Disorder (PTSD): Experiencing flashbacks, anxiety, and other symptoms related to trauma exposure.

- Cumulative Stress: The buildup of stress over time from repeated exposure to traumatic incidents.

6.1.2 High-Pressure Situations

The high-pressure environment of law enforcement can contribute to:

- Chronic Stress: Persistent stress resulting from the demands and responsibilities of the job.

- Burnout: Physical, emotional, and mental exhaustion caused by prolonged exposure to stressful situations.

6.1.3 Personal and Professional Balance

Balancing personal life with professional responsibilities can be challenging for officers, leading to:

- Family Strain: Struggles in personal relationships due to the demands of the job.

- Work-Life Imbalance: Difficulty in maintaining a healthy balance between work and personal life.

6.2 Providing Emotional and Mental Health Support

Police chaplains offer various forms of emotional and mental health support to help officers cope with their stresses and traumas. This support includes individual counseling, group sessions, and crisis intervention.

6.2.1 Individual Counseling

One-on-one counseling sessions provide officers with a safe and confidential space to discuss their concerns and receive personalized support. This can include:

- Emotional Support: Helping officers process their feelings and emotions related to their work.

- Coping Strategies: Teaching techniques for managing stress, anxiety, and trauma.

- Spiritual Guidance: Offering faith-based support and guidance tailored to the officer's beliefs and values.

6.2.2 Group Support Sessions

Group support sessions foster a sense of community and shared understanding among officers. These sessions can involve:

- Peer Support: Encouraging officers to share their experiences and offer mutual support.

- Stress Management Workshops: Teaching techniques for managing stress and improving mental health.

- Discussion Groups: Facilitating open discussions on topics such as trauma, resilience, and work-life balance.

6.2.3 Crisis Intervention

During critical incidents, chaplains provide immediate support to help officers manage their emotional and psychological responses. This includes:

- On-Scene Support: Offering comfort and reassurance at the scene of a critical incident.

- Follow-Up Care: Providing ongoing counseling and support to address the long-term impacts of trauma.

- Resource Referral: Connecting officers with mental health professionals and additional support services.

6.3 Strategies for Supporting Mental Health

Effective support for officers' mental health requires specific strategies and approaches. Chaplains use various methods to address the mental health challenges faced by law enforcement officers.

6.3.1 Building Trust and Rapport

Building trust and rapport with officers is essential for effective support. This involves:

- Regular Interaction: Maintaining a visible and approachable presence within the department.

- Confidentiality: Ensuring that all conversations and counseling sessions remain confidential.

- Empathy and Understanding: Demonstrating genuine care and concern for the well-being of officers.

6.3.2 Promoting Resilience

Chaplains help officers develop resilience to better cope with stress and trauma. This includes:

- Resilience Training: Teaching techniques for building emotional and psychological resilience.

- Encouraging Self-Care: Promoting practices such as regular exercise, healthy eating, and adequate rest.

- Mindfulness Practices: Introducing mindfulness techniques to help officers stay grounded and focused.

6.3.3 Addressing Stigma

Chaplains work to reduce the stigma associated with seeking mental health support. This involves:

- Raising Awareness: Educating officers about the importance of mental health and the benefits of seeking support.

- Normalizing Conversations: Creating an environment where discussing mental health issues is accepted and encouraged.

- Leading by Example: Encouraging officers to prioritize their mental health through their actions and words.

6.4 The Impact of Chaplain Support on Officer Well-Being

The support provided by chaplains has a profound impact on the mental and emotional well-being of law enforcement officers. This support contributes to:

6.4.1 Improved Mental Health

Chaplains help officers manage stress, anxiety, and trauma, leading to:

- Reduced Symptoms of PTSD: Decreasing the frequency and intensity of PTSD symptoms through effective counseling and support.

- Lower Stress Levels: Helping officers develop coping strategies to manage chronic stress and prevent burnout.

6.4.2 Enhanced Job Performance

Officers who receive emotional and mental health support are better equipped to perform their duties effectively. This includes:

- Improved Focus and Decision-Making: Reducing the impact of stress on cognitive functions and decision-making abilities.

- Increased Job Satisfaction: Enhancing officers' overall job satisfaction and commitment to their work.

6.4.3 Strengthened Relationships

Chaplains support officers in maintaining healthy personal and professional relationships. This leads to:

- Better Family Dynamics: Helping officers balance their work and personal lives, improving family relationships.

- Positive Workplace Environment: Fostering a supportive and collaborative work environment among officers.

6.5 Case Studies and Real-Life Examples

Real-life examples illustrate the significant impact of chaplain support on officers' mental and emotional well-being.

6.5.1 Supporting an Officer with PTSD

Officer Mark struggled with PTSD after being involved in a traumatic incident. Chaplain Sarah provided regular counseling sessions, helping Mark process his trauma and develop coping strategies. Over time, Mark's PTSD symptoms decreased, and he was able to return to his duties with greater resilience and confidence.

6.5.2 Facilitating a Stress Management Workshop

Chaplain John organized a stress management workshop for officers, teaching techniques such as deep breathing, mindfulness, and time management. The workshop received positive feedback, with many officers reporting improved stress levels and overall well-being.

6.5.3 Providing Crisis Intervention After a Critical Incident

Following a critical incident involving a fatal shooting, Chaplain Lisa was on the scene to provide immediate support to the affected officers. She offered words of comfort, helped officers manage their initial shock and grief, and provided ongoing counseling to address the long-term impacts of the trauma.

6.6 Essential Qualities for Supporting Mental Health

Supporting the mental and emotional well-being of officers requires specific qualities and skills, including:

6.6.1 Compassion

Compassion is essential for understanding and addressing the emotional needs of officers. Chaplains must demonstrate genuine care and empathy.

6.6.2 Confidentiality

Maintaining confidentiality is crucial for building trust and providing effective support. Chaplains must ensure that all conversations and counseling sessions remain private.

6.6.3 Resilience

Resilience is important for managing the emotional toll of their work. Chaplains must develop strategies for maintaining their well-being and preventing burnout.

6.6.4 Effective Communication

Effective communication skills are vital for providing support, offering guidance, and coordinating with other mental health professionals. Chaplains must be able to articulate their thoughts and emotions clearly and empathetically.

6.7 Conclusion

Police chaplains play a crucial role in supporting the mental and emotional well-being of officers, helping them cope with the stresses and traumas of their work. Through individual counseling, group sessions, crisis intervention, and resilience training, chaplains provide essential support that enhances officers' mental health, job performance, and relationships. By employing effective strategies, building trust, and practicing self-care, chaplains make a significant impact on the overall well-being of the law enforcement community.

FAMILY SUPPORT SERVICES

Introduction

The families of police officers also benefit from the services of chaplains, who offer counseling and support to help them navigate the unique challenges of having a loved one in law enforcement. This chapter explores the various ways chaplains provide support to the families of officers, the strategies they use to address the specific needs of these families, and the impact of their work on the overall well-being of law enforcement families.

6.1 Understanding the Challenges Faced by Police Families

Families of police officers face unique challenges due to the demanding nature of law enforcement work. These challenges can include dealing with the stress and unpredictability of the job, managing the impact of critical incidents, and maintaining family dynamics despite irregular schedules and high-pressure environments.

6.1.1 Stress and Unpredictability

The unpredictable nature of police work can lead to:

- Anxiety and Worry: Constant concern for the safety of their loved ones.

- Irregular Schedules: Difficulty in planning family activities due to unpredictable work hours.

- Emotional Strain: Managing the emotional highs and lows associated with the risks and demands of the job.

6.1.2 Impact of Critical Incidents

Families are often affected by critical incidents involving their loved ones, leading to:

- Trauma and Grief: Coping with the trauma and grief resulting from critical incidents such as shootings, accidents, or line-of-duty deaths.

- Secondary Trauma: Experiencing emotional distress from hearing about or witnessing the aftermath of traumatic events.

6.1.3 Maintaining Family Dynamics

Balancing family dynamics with the demands of law enforcement work can be challenging, leading to:

- Strained Relationships: Tension and conflicts arising from the stress and demands of the job.

- Parenting Challenges: Difficulties in co-parenting and maintaining a stable home environment.

6.2 Providing Family Support Services

Police chaplains offer a range of family support services to help families navigate these challenges. These services include individual and family counseling, support groups, and crisis intervention.

6.2.1 Individual and Family Counseling

Chaplains provide counseling to individual family members and entire families, offering a safe and confidential space to discuss their concerns and receive support. This includes:

- Emotional Support: Helping family members process their emotions and cope with stress and anxiety.

- Communication Strategies: Teaching effective communication techniques to improve family relationships and resolve conflicts.

- Parenting Support: Offering guidance on parenting challenges and strategies for maintaining a stable home environment.

6.2.2 Support Groups

Support groups provide a sense of community and shared understanding among police families. These groups can involve:

- Peer Support: Encouraging families to share their experiences and offer mutual support.

- Educational Workshops: Providing information on topics such as stress management, trauma recovery, and resilience.

- Discussion Groups: Facilitating open discussions on the unique challenges faced by police families and strategies for coping.

6.2.3 Crisis Intervention

During critical incidents, chaplains provide immediate and ongoing support to affected families. This includes:

- On-Scene Support: Offering comfort and reassurance to families during critical incidents.

- Hospital Visits: Visiting injured officers and their families in the hospital to provide support and information.

- Follow-Up Care: Ensuring ongoing counseling and support to address the long-term impacts of trauma and grief.

6.3 Strategies for Supporting Police Families

Effective support for police families requires specific strategies and approaches. Chaplains use various methods to address the unique needs and challenges faced by these families.

6.3.1 Building Trust and Rapport

Building trust and rapport with families is essential for effective support. This involves:

- Regular Interaction: Maintaining a visible and approachable presence within the community of police families.

- Confidentiality: Ensuring that all conversations and counseling sessions remain confidential.

- Empathy and Understanding: Demonstrating genuine care and concern for the well-being of families.

6.3.2 Promoting Resilience

Chaplains help families develop resilience to better cope with the stresses and challenges of law enforcement life. This includes:

- Resilience Training: Teaching techniques for building emotional and psychological resilience.

- Encouraging Self-Care: Promoting practices such as regular exercise, healthy eating, and adequate rest.

- Mindfulness Practices: Introducing mindfulness techniques to help families stay grounded and focused.

6.3.3 Addressing Stigma

Chaplains work to reduce the stigma associated with seeking support. This involves:

- Raising Awareness: Educating families about the importance of mental health and the benefits of seeking support.

- Normalizing Conversations: Creating an environment where discussing mental health issues is accepted and encouraged.

- Leading by Example: Encouraging families to prioritize their mental health through their actions and words.

6.4 The Impact of Chaplain Support on Police Families

The support provided by chaplains has a profound impact on the well-being of police families. This support contributes to:

6.4.1 Improved Family Dynamics

Chaplains help families improve their relationships and communication, leading to:

- Stronger Bonds: Enhancing the emotional connections between family members.

- Better Communication: Teaching effective communication strategies to resolve conflicts and express emotions.

6.4.2 Enhanced Resilience

Chaplains help families develop resilience, enabling them to cope more effectively with the challenges of law enforcement life. This includes:

- Increased Coping Skills: Teaching techniques for managing stress and anxiety.

- Greater Emotional Stability: Helping families maintain emotional stability during challenging times.

6.4.3 Support During Critical Incidents

Chaplains provide crucial support during critical incidents, helping families navigate the immediate and long-term impacts of trauma and grief. This includes:

- Immediate Comfort: Offering immediate comfort and reassurance during critical incidents.

- Ongoing Counseling: Providing ongoing counseling and support to help families process their experiences and heal.

6.5 Case Studies and Real-Life Examples

Real-life examples illustrate the significant impact of chaplain support on police families.

6.5.1 Supporting a Family After a Line-of-Duty Death

After Officer James was killed in the line of duty, Chaplain Lisa provided immediate support to his family. She offered comfort and reassurance, helped them navigate the funeral arrangements, and provided ongoing counseling to address their grief and trauma. Chaplain Lisa's support helped the family find strength and resilience during a challenging time.

6.5.2 Facilitating a Family Support Group

Chaplain John organized a support group for police families, providing a safe space for families to share their experiences and offer mutual support. The group included educational workshops on stress management and resilience, as well as open discussions on the unique challenges faced by police families. The support group helped families build a sense of community and shared understanding.

6.5.3 Providing Crisis Intervention During a Critical Incident

Following a critical incident involving an officer-involved shooting, Chaplain Sarah provided immediate support to the affected officer's family. She visited the hospital to offer comfort and information, coordinated with medical staff, and provided ongoing counseling to help the family cope with the trauma and uncertainty. Chaplain Sarah's support was crucial in helping the family navigate the aftermath of the incident.

6.6 Essential Qualities for Supporting Police Families

Supporting the families of police officers requires specific qualities and skills, including:

6.6.1 Compassion

Compassion is essential for understanding and addressing the emotional needs of families. Chaplains must demonstrate genuine care and empathy.

6.6.2 Confidentiality

Maintaining confidentiality is crucial for building trust and providing effective support. Chaplains must ensure that all conversations and counseling sessions remain private.

6.6.3 Resilience

Resilience is important for managing the emotional toll of their work. Chaplains must develop strategies for maintaining their well-being and preventing burnout.

6.6.4 Effective Communication

Effective communication skills are vital for providing support, offering guidance, and coordinating with other support services. Chaplains must be able to articulate their thoughts and emotions clearly and empathetically.

6.7 Conclusion

Police chaplains play a crucial role in supporting the families of officers, helping them navigate the unique challenges of having a loved one in law enforcement. Through individual and family counseling, support groups, and crisis intervention, chaplains provide essential support that enhances family dynamics, resilience, and overall well-being. By employing effective strategies, building trust, and practicing self-care, chaplains make a significant impact on the well-being of police families.

This chapter has explored the various ways chaplains provide support to police families, the strategies they use to address their specific needs, and the impact of their work on the overall well-being of law enforcement families. Subsequent chapters will delve deeper into other aspects of police chaplaincy, including the challenges and rewards of this essential vocation.

PROVIDING A SAFE SPACE FOR OFFICERS

Introduction

Creating a safe and confidential space for officers to express their concerns and seek guidance is a key aspect of police chaplaincy. This environment is crucial for fostering trust, encouraging open communication, and providing effective support. This chapter explores the importance of providing a safe space, the strategies chaplains use to create and maintain this environment, and the impact of these efforts on the well-being of law enforcement officers.

6.1 The Importance of a Safe Space

A safe space allows officers to openly discuss their personal and professional challenges without fear of judgment or repercussions. This is vital for several reasons:

6.1.1 Encouraging Open Communication

Open communication is essential for addressing issues that may affect an officer's mental and emotional well-being. A safe space encourages officers to share their concerns, which is the first step in receiving the help they need.

6.1.2 Building Trust

Trust is the foundation of effective chaplaincy. When officers feel secure in their interactions with chaplains, they are more likely to seek support and follow through with recommended actions.

6.1.3 Reducing Stigma

Providing a confidential environment helps reduce the stigma associated with seeking mental health support. When officers know their privacy will be respected, they are more likely to discuss sensitive issues.

6.2 Strategies for Creating a Safe Space

Chaplains use various strategies to create and maintain a safe space for officers. These strategies include ensuring confidentiality, demonstrating empathy, and maintaining a non-judgmental attitude.

6.2.1 Ensuring Confidentiality

Confidentiality is paramount in building trust and providing a safe space. Chaplains must:

- Clarify Boundaries: Clearly explain the limits of confidentiality and under what circumstances information may be disclosed.

- Protect Privacy: Ensure that all conversations and records are kept private and secure.

- Follow Ethical Guidelines: Adhere to professional ethical standards to maintain confidentiality and trust.

6.2.2 Demonstrating Empathy

Empathy is essential for understanding and addressing the concerns of officers. Chaplains must:

- Active Listening: Listen attentively without interrupting, showing genuine interest in what the officer is saying.

- Reflective Responses: Reflect back what the officer has said to show understanding and validation.

- Compassionate Interaction: Show compassion and understanding, demonstrating that they genuinely care about the officer's well-being.

6.2.3 Maintaining a Non-Judgmental Attitude

A non-judgmental attitude helps officers feel safe and respected. Chaplains must:

- Avoid Judgment: Refrain from passing judgment on the officer's actions or feelings.

- Supportive Environment: Create an environment where officers feel comfortable sharing their thoughts and experiences.

- Encouraging Expression: Encourage officers to express themselves freely, without fear of criticism.

6.3 Providing Accessible and Welcoming Spaces

The physical and emotional accessibility of the chaplain's office or meeting space also plays a role in creating a safe environment. Chaplains should ensure that their space is welcoming and conducive to open communication.

6.3.1 Comfortable Setting

A comfortable setting can help put officers at ease. This includes:

- Private Space: Providing a private, quiet space where officers can speak without being overheard.

- Inviting Atmosphere: Creating a warm and inviting atmosphere with comfortable seating and calming decor.

- Accessibility: Ensuring the space is easily accessible to all officers, including those with disabilities.

6.3.2 Flexible Availability

Flexibility in scheduling is important for accommodating the varying shifts and busy schedules of officers. This includes:

- Flexible Hours: Offering appointments outside of traditional office hours to accommodate shift work.

- On-Call Support: Being available for urgent support when needed.

- Proactive Outreach: Reaching out to officers who may need support but are hesitant to seek it out.

6.4 Building and Maintaining Trust

Building and maintaining trust is an ongoing process that requires consistent effort and dedication. Chaplains must continuously demonstrate their commitment to supporting officers.

6.4.1 Consistent Presence

Being consistently present and available helps build trust over time. This includes:

- Regular Interaction: Participating in daily briefings, roll calls, and other department activities.

- Visibility: Being a visible and approachable presence within the department.

- Reliability: Following through on commitments and being dependable.

6.4.2 Follow-Up Care

Providing follow-up care demonstrates a chaplain's ongoing commitment to an officer's well-being. This includes:

- Regular Check-Ins: Checking in with officers after initial consultations to see how they are doing.

- Ongoing Support: Offering continuous support and counseling as needed.

- Resource Connection: Connecting officers with additional resources and support services.

6.5 The Impact of a Safe Space on Officer Well-Being

Providing a safe space has a significant impact on the overall well-being of law enforcement officers. This support can lead to improved mental health, better job performance, and enhanced personal relationships.

6.5.1 Improved Mental Health

A safe space encourages officers to address their mental health concerns, leading to:

- Reduced Stress and Anxiety: Helping officers manage stress and anxiety through effective counseling and support.

- Enhanced Coping Skills: Teaching officers coping strategies to deal with the challenges of their work.

- Prevention of Burnout: Providing support to prevent burnout and promote resilience.

6.5.2 Better Job Performance

When officers feel supported, their job performance improves. This includes:

- Increased Focus: Reducing the impact of personal and professional stress on their ability to perform their duties.

- Better Decision-Making: Enhancing cognitive functions and decision-making abilities through improved mental health.

- Higher Job Satisfaction: Increasing overall job satisfaction and commitment to their work.

6.5.3 Enhanced Personal Relationships

Support from chaplains can also improve officers' personal relationships. This includes:

- Stronger Family Bonds: Helping officers navigate the challenges of balancing work and family life.

- Improved Communication: Teaching effective communication strategies for resolving conflicts and expressing emotions.

- Supportive Networks: Building a supportive network within the department and the broader community.

6.6 Case Studies and Real-Life Examples

Real-life examples illustrate the significant impact of providing a safe space for officers.

6.6.1 Supporting an Officer Through Personal Crisis

Officer Jane was experiencing significant stress due to personal issues and felt overwhelmed by her duties. Chaplain Mike provided a safe and confidential space for Jane to discuss her concerns. Through regular counseling sessions, Mike helped Jane develop coping strategies and manage her stress, leading to improved well-being and job performance.

6.6.2 Building Trust Over Time

Chaplain Emily made a point to attend daily briefings and roll calls, becoming a familiar and trusted presence within the department. Over time, officers began to feel comfortable approaching her with their concerns, knowing they could trust her to provide confidential and compassionate support.

6.6.3 Creating a Welcoming Environment

Chaplain John transformed his office into a welcoming and comfortable space, complete with calming decor and comfortable seating. He ensured his office was accessible to all officers and maintained flexible hours to accommodate their schedules. This inviting environment encouraged more officers to seek support.

6.7 Essential Qualities for Creating a Safe Space

Creating a safe and confidential space for officers requires specific qualities and skills, including:

6.7.1 Compassion

Compassion is essential for understanding and addressing the emotional needs of officers. Chaplains must demonstrate genuine care and empathy.

6.7.2 Confidentiality

Maintaining confidentiality is crucial for building trust and providing effective support. Chaplains must ensure that all conversations and counseling sessions remain private.

6.7.3 Resilience

Resilience is important for managing the emotional toll of their work. Chaplains must develop strategies for maintaining their well-being and preventing burnout.

6.7.4 Effective Communication

Effective communication skills are vital for providing support, offering guidance, and coordinating with other support services. Chaplains must be able to articulate their thoughts and emotions clearly and empathetically.

6.8 Conclusion

Creating a safe and confidential space for officers to express their concerns and seek guidance is a key aspect of police chaplaincy. By ensuring confidentiality, demonstrating empathy, and maintaining a non-judgmental attitude, chaplains foster an environment of trust and open communication. The support provided in this safe space has a profound impact on the mental health, job performance, and personal relationships of law enforcement officers.

CHAPTER 07

COMMUNITY OUTREACH AND ENGAGEMENT

Building Bridges with the Community

Police chaplains play a vital role in fostering positive relationships between law enforcement and the community. Through various outreach and engagement activities, they promote mutual understanding, trust, and cooperation. This chapter explores the importance of community outreach and engagement, the strategies chaplains use to build bridges, and the impact of these efforts on both the police force and the community.

7.1 The Importance of Community Outreach and Engagement

Community outreach and engagement are essential for several reasons. They help to build trust, reduce misunderstandings, and create a sense of partnership between law enforcement and the community.

7.1.1 Building Trust

Trust is the foundation of effective law enforcement. When the community trusts the police, cooperation and compliance increase, leading to safer neighborhoods.

- Transparency: Open communication and transparency in police activities foster trust.

- Accountability: Demonstrating accountability through community engagement builds credibility.

7.1.2 Reducing Misunderstandings

Misunderstandings between law enforcement and the community can lead to tension and conflict. Effective outreach helps to clarify the role and actions of the police.

- Educational Programs: Providing information about police procedures and the legal system.

- Dialogue Opportunities: Creating spaces for open dialogue where community members can express their concerns and ask questions.

7.1.3 Creating Partnerships

Engagement activities help to create a sense of partnership between the police and the community, encouraging collaborative efforts to address local issues.

- Collaborative Initiatives: Working together on community projects and safety initiatives.

- Resource Sharing: Leveraging community resources and support to enhance public safety.

7.2 Strategies for Community Outreach and Engagement

Police chaplains use various strategies to engage with the community and build positive relationships. These strategies include organizing community events, participating in educational programs, and facilitating interfaith collaborations.

7.2.1 Organizing Community Events

Community events provide opportunities for positive interactions between law enforcement and community members.

- Public Safety Fairs: Organizing fairs to educate the community about safety practices and police services.

- Family Days: Hosting events that bring officers and their families together with community members for recreational activities.

- Cultural Celebrations: Participating in cultural events and celebrations to show respect and appreciation for the diversity within the community.

7.2.2 Participating in Educational Programs

Educational programs help to inform the community about law enforcement practices and promote understanding.

- School Visits: Visiting schools to educate students about the role of the police and promote safety.

- Workshops and Seminars: Leading workshops on topics such as crime prevention, emergency preparedness, and conflict resolution.

- Youth Programs: Engaging with youth through mentorship programs, sports activities, and leadership training.

7.2.3 Facilitating Interfaith Collaborations

Interfaith collaborations promote inclusivity and respect for diverse religious beliefs within the community.

- Interfaith Dialogues: Organizing dialogues and forums that bring together leaders from various faith communities to discuss common concerns and promote mutual understanding.

- Joint Community Projects: Collaborating on community service projects that address local needs and foster cooperation among different religious groups.

- Cultural Competency Training: Providing training for officers on cultural and religious sensitivity to enhance their interactions with diverse community members.

7.3 The Impact of Community Outreach and Engagement

The efforts of police chaplains in community outreach and engagement have a significant impact on both the police force and the community. These impacts include enhanced public trust, improved community safety, and stronger community-police partnerships.

7.3.1 Enhanced Public Trust

Through consistent and positive interactions, chaplains help to build and maintain public trust in law enforcement.

- Positive Perception: Regular engagement activities improve the public's perception of the police.

- Transparency and Accountability: Open communication and visible accountability measures foster trust and confidence in law enforcement.

7.3.2 Improved Community Safety

Engaging with the community helps to identify and address local safety concerns, leading to a safer environment for all.

- Proactive Policing: Collaborative efforts enable proactive policing strategies that address root causes of crime.

- Community Involvement: Encouraging community members to participate in safety initiatives enhances the effectiveness of these programs.

7.3.3 Stronger Community-Police Partnerships

Effective outreach efforts create stronger partnerships between the police and the community, leading to more effective problem-solving and resource-sharing.

- Collaborative Problem-Solving: Working together to address community issues results in more sustainable solutions.

- Resource Optimization: Leveraging community resources and support enhances the capabilities of law enforcement.

7.4 Case Studies and Real-Life Examples

Real-life examples illustrate the significant impact of community outreach and engagement efforts by police chaplains.

7.4.1 Organizing a Community Safety Fair

Chaplain Jessica organized a community safety fair that brought together local law enforcement, fire departments, and health services. The event featured demonstrations, informational booths, and activities for children. This fair helped to educate the community about safety practices, build positive relationships, and foster trust in public safety officials.

7.4.2 Leading a Youth Mentorship Program

Chaplain David developed a mentorship program for at-risk youth, pairing them with police officers who provided guidance, support, and positive role models. The program included regular meetings, recreational activities, and educational workshops. This initiative helped to reduce juvenile delinquency, improve school performance, and build trust between young people and the police.

7.4.3 Facilitating an Interfaith Dialogue

Chaplain Maria facilitated an interfaith dialogue that brought together leaders from different religious communities to discuss common concerns and promote mutual understanding. The dialogue led to several joint community service projects, including a neighborhood clean-up and a food drive. These collaborative efforts helped to strengthen community bonds and foster a sense of unity.

7.5 Essential Qualities for Effective Community Engagement

Effective community engagement requires specific qualities and skills, including:

7.5.1 Empathy

Empathy is essential for understanding the concerns and perspectives of community members. Chaplains must demonstrate genuine care and concern for the well-being of the community.

7.5.2 Communication Skills

Effective communication skills are vital for building relationships, facilitating dialogue, and conveying important information. Chaplains must be able to articulate their thoughts and emotions clearly and empathetically.

7.5.3 Cultural Competency

Cultural competency is important for engaging with diverse communities. Chaplains must understand and respect the cultural and religious beliefs of the communities they serve.

7.5.4 Collaboration

Collaboration is key to successful community engagement. Chaplains must be able to work effectively with law enforcement, community leaders, and organizations to achieve common goals.

7.6 Conclusion

Police chaplains play a vital role in fostering positive relationships between law enforcement and the community through outreach and engagement activities. By organizing community events, participating in educational programs, and facilitating interfaith collaborations, chaplains promote mutual understanding, trust, and cooperation. These efforts have a significant impact on both the police force and the community, leading to enhanced public trust, improved community safety, and stronger community-police partnerships.

FAITH-BASE INITIATIVES

Introduction

Many police chaplains lead faith-based initiatives that benefit both the police force and the community. These initiatives often include youth programs, community service projects, and various outreach activities. By integrating faith-based principles into their work, chaplains provide holistic support that addresses the spiritual, emotional, and physical needs of individuals and the community. This chapter explores the types of faith-based initiatives led by chaplains, their impact, and the strategies used to implement these programs effectively.

7.1 Types of Faith-Based Initiatives

Faith-based initiatives led by police chaplains are diverse and tailored to meet the specific needs of the police force and the community. These initiatives often include youth programs, community service projects, and support groups.

7.1.1 Youth Programs

Youth programs aim to provide positive role models, support, and guidance to young people. These programs often focus on:

- Mentorship: Pairing youth with police officers and community leaders who can provide guidance and support.

- Educational Workshops: Offering workshops on topics such as leadership, decision-making, and conflict resolution.

- Recreational Activities: Organizing sports, arts, and other recreational activities to promote healthy development.

7.1.2 Community Service Projects

Community service projects involve law enforcement officers and community members working together to address local needs. These projects often include:

- Neighborhood Clean-Ups: Organizing clean-up efforts to improve the appearance and safety of local neighborhoods.

- Food Drives: Collecting and distributing food to those in need within the community.

- Housing Repairs: Assisting with home repairs and maintenance for elderly or low-income residents.

7.1.3 Support Groups

Support groups provide a safe and supportive environment for individuals to share their experiences and receive encouragement. These groups often focus on:

- Grief Support: Offering support to individuals and families dealing with loss.

- Addiction Recovery: Providing a faith-based approach to addiction recovery, including counseling and peer support.

- Stress Management: Helping officers and community members manage stress through group discussions and relaxation techniques.

7.2 Implementing Faith-Based Initiatives

Effective implementation of faith-based initiatives requires careful planning, collaboration, and community engagement. Chaplains use various strategies to ensure the success of these programs.

7.2.1 Needs Assessment

Conducting a needs assessment helps identify the specific needs and priorities of the police force and the community. This involves:

- Surveys and Interviews: Gathering input from officers, community members, and local organizations.

- Data Analysis: Analyzing data to identify trends and areas of need.

- Community Meetings: Hosting meetings to discuss findings and gather additional insights.

7.2.2 Collaborative Partnerships

Building collaborative partnerships with local organizations, faith communities, and other stakeholders is crucial for the success of faith-based initiatives. This involves:

- Networking: Establishing connections with potential partners and collaborators.

- Resource Sharing: Pooling resources and expertise to enhance program effectiveness.

- Joint Planning: Collaborating on the planning and implementation of initiatives to ensure they meet the needs of all stakeholders.

7.2.3 Volunteer Engagement

Engaging volunteers is essential for the successful implementation of faith-based initiatives. This involves:

- Recruitment: Actively recruiting volunteers from within the police force, faith communities, and the broader community.

- Training: Providing training to ensure volunteers are well-prepared and confident in their roles.

- Recognition: Recognizing and celebrating the contributions of volunteers to maintain motivation and engagement.

7.2.4 Continuous Evaluation

Continuous evaluation helps ensure that faith-based initiatives are meeting their goals and making a positive impact. This involves:

- Monitoring Progress: Regularly tracking the progress of initiatives and assessing their effectiveness.

- Feedback Mechanisms: Gathering feedback from participants, volunteers, and partners to identify areas for improvement.

- Adjustments: Making necessary adjustments to improve program outcomes and address any challenges.

7.3 The Impact of Faith-Based Initiatives

Faith-based initiatives led by police chaplains have a significant impact on both the police force and the community. These initiatives contribute to enhanced community relations, improved individual well-being, and stronger support networks.

7.3.1 Enhanced Community Relations

Faith-based initiatives foster positive relationships between law enforcement and the community. This includes:

- Building Trust: Creating opportunities for positive interactions and collaboration between officers and community members.

- Promoting Understanding: Increasing mutual understanding and respect through shared experiences and dialogue.

- Encouraging Cooperation: Encouraging community members to work together with law enforcement to address local issues.

7.3.2 Improved Individual Well-Being

These initiatives address the holistic needs of individuals, contributing to their overall well-being. This includes:

- Emotional Support: Providing emotional and spiritual support to individuals facing challenges.

- Skill Development: Helping individuals develop skills and knowledge that contribute to their personal and professional growth.

- Sense of Purpose: Encouraging individuals to engage in meaningful activities that promote a sense of purpose and fulfillment.

7.3.3 Stronger Support Networks

Faith-based initiatives help build stronger support networks within the community. This includes:

- Peer Support: Fostering connections and support among individuals with similar experiences and challenges.

- Community Involvement: Encouraging community members to take an active role in supporting one another.

- Collaborative Efforts: Strengthening collaboration between law enforcement, faith communities, and other local organizations.

7.4 Case Studies and Real-Life Examples

Real-life examples illustrate the significant impact of faith-based initiatives led by police chaplains.

7.4.1 Youth Mentorship Program

Chaplain Robert implemented a youth mentorship program that paired at-risk youth with police officers and community leaders. The program included regular mentorship meetings, educational workshops, and recreational activities. As a result, participating youth showed improved school performance, increased self-esteem, and a reduction in delinquent behavior.

7.4.2 Community Clean-Up Project

Chaplain Maria organized a community clean-up project in collaboration with local churches and civic organizations. The project brought together officers, community members, and volunteers to clean up local parks and streets. This initiative not only improved the physical environment but also strengthened community bonds and fostered a sense of pride and ownership.

7.4.3 Addiction Recovery Support Group

Chaplain David started an addiction recovery support group that provided faith-based counseling and peer support to individuals struggling with substance abuse. The group met weekly and offered a supportive environment for participants to share their experiences and work towards recovery. Many participants reported significant progress in their recovery journeys and credited the group with providing essential support and encouragement.

7.5 Essential Qualities for Leading Faith-Based Initiatives

Leading successful faith-based initiatives requires specific qualities and skills, including:

7.5.1 Compassion

Compassion is essential for understanding and addressing the needs of individuals and the community. Chaplains must demonstrate genuine care and empathy in their interactions.

7.5.2 Leadership

Effective leadership is crucial for organizing and guiding faith-based initiatives. Chaplains must be able to inspire and motivate others, manage resources, and coordinate activities.

7.5.3 Collaboration

Collaboration is key to successful faith-based initiatives. Chaplains must be able to work effectively with a diverse range of partners and stakeholders.

7.5.4 Flexibility

Flexibility is important for adapting to changing circumstances and needs. Chaplains must be able to adjust their plans and strategies to ensure the success of their initiatives.

7.6 Conclusion

Faith-based initiatives led by police chaplains provide valuable support to both the police force and the community. Through youth programs, community service projects, and support groups, chaplains address the holistic needs of individuals and foster positive relationships between law enforcement and the community. By implementing effective strategies and demonstrating essential qualities, chaplains make a significant impact on the well-being of individuals and the strength of community support networks.

COLLABORATIVE PROGRAMS WITH LOCAL CHRUCH AND ORGANIZATIONS

Introduction

Partnerships with local churches and organizations enhance the reach and impact of police chaplaincy programs by providing additional resources and support. These collaborations enable chaplains to extend their services to a broader audience, address diverse needs, and foster a sense of community. This chapter explores the benefits of collaborative programs, the strategies for building and maintaining partnerships, and the impact of these efforts on both the police force and the community.

7.1 Benefits of Collaborative Programs

Collaborative programs with local churches and organizations offer numerous benefits, including increased resources, broader outreach, and enhanced community relationships.

7.1.1 Increased Resources

Collaborating with local churches and organizations provides access to additional resources that can enhance the effectiveness of chaplaincy programs. These resources include:

- Funding: Financial support for programs and initiatives.

- Volunteers: Additional manpower to support events and activities.

- Facilities: Access to meeting spaces, event venues, and other facilities.

7.1.2 Broader Outreach

Partnerships with local churches and organizations enable chaplains to reach a wider audience and address diverse needs within the community. This includes:

- Community Networks: Leveraging existing networks and relationships to reach more people.

- Targeted Programs: Developing programs that address specific needs and demographics.

- Enhanced Communication: Utilizing various communication channels to promote programs and events.

7.1.3 Enhanced Community Relationships

Collaborative programs help to strengthen relationships between the police force and the community by promoting mutual understanding and cooperation. This includes:

- Building Trust: Demonstrating a commitment to community well-being through joint efforts.

- Fostering Unity: Encouraging collaboration and partnership among different community groups.

- Promoting Positive Interactions: Creating opportunities for positive interactions between officers and community members.

7.2 Strategies for Building and Maintaining Partnerships

Building and maintaining successful partnerships with local churches and organizations require intentional effort and effective strategies. These strategies include identifying potential partners, establishing clear goals, and fostering ongoing communication.

7.2.1 Identifying Potential Partners

The first step in building collaborative programs is identifying potential partners who share similar values and goals. This involves:

- Research: Identifying local churches, faith-based organizations, and community groups with a history of community engagement.

- Networking: Attending community events, meetings, and forums to connect with potential partners.

- Referrals: Seeking recommendations from officers, community members, and existing partners.

7.2.2 Establishing Clear Goals and Objectives

Establishing clear goals and objectives for collaborative programs helps ensure that all partners are aligned and working towards a common purpose. This includes:

- Defining Objectives: Clearly outlining the goals and desired outcomes of the partnership.

- Setting Expectations: Establishing roles, responsibilities, and expectations for each partner.

- Developing a Plan: Creating a detailed plan that outlines the steps and timeline for achieving the goals.

7.2.3 Fostering Ongoing Communication

Effective communication is essential for maintaining successful partnerships. This involves:

- Regular Meetings: Scheduling regular meetings to discuss progress, address challenges, and plan future activities.

- Open Dialogue: Encouraging open and honest communication among partners.

- Feedback Mechanisms: Implementing mechanisms for gathering and incorporating feedback from all partners.

7.3 Types of Collaborative Programs

Collaborative programs with local churches and organizations can take many forms, each tailored to meet specific community needs. These programs often include community service projects, educational workshops, and support groups.

7.3.1 Community Service Projects

Community service projects involve joint efforts between the police force, local churches, and organizations to address local needs. Examples include:

- Food Drives: Collecting and distributing food to those in need.

- Neighborhood Clean-Ups: Organizing clean-up efforts to improve local neighborhoods.

- Housing Repairs: Assisting with home repairs and maintenance for elderly or low-income residents.

7.3.2 Educational Workshops

Educational workshops provide valuable information and resources to the community. Examples include:

- Safety Workshops: Offering workshops on topics such as personal safety, emergency preparedness, and crime prevention.

- Health and Wellness: Providing information on physical and mental health, nutrition, and wellness practices.

- Youth Development: Conducting workshops on leadership, decision-making, and conflict resolution for young people.

7.3.3 Support Groups

Support groups offer a safe and supportive environment for individuals to share their experiences and receive encouragement. Examples include:

- Grief Support: Providing support to individuals and families dealing with loss.

- Addiction Recovery: Offering faith-based support for individuals struggling with substance abuse.

- Stress Management: Helping officers and community members manage stress through group discussions and relaxation techniques.

7.4 The Impact of Collaborative Programs

Collaborative programs with local churches and organizations have a significant impact on both the police force and the community. These impacts include enhanced community relationships, improved individual well-being, and stronger support networks.

7.4.1 Enhanced Community Relationships

Collaborative programs help to build trust and foster positive relationships between law enforcement and the community. This includes:

- Building Trust: Demonstrating a commitment to community well-being through joint efforts.

- Promoting Unity: Encouraging collaboration and partnership among different community groups.

- Creating Positive Interactions: Providing opportunities for positive interactions between officers and community members.

7.4.2 Improved Individual Well-Being

These programs address the holistic needs of individuals, contributing to their overall well-being. This includes:

- Emotional Support: Providing emotional and spiritual support to individuals facing challenges.

- Skill Development: Helping individuals develop skills and knowledge that contribute to their personal and professional growth.

- Sense of Purpose: Encouraging individuals to engage in meaningful activities that promote a sense of purpose and fulfillment.

7.4.3 Stronger Support Networks

Collaborative programs help build stronger support networks within the community. This includes:

- Peer Support: Fostering connections and support among individuals with similar experiences and challenges.

- Community Involvement: Encouraging community members to take an active role in supporting one another.

- Collaborative Efforts: Strengthening collaboration between law enforcement, faith communities, and other local organizations.

7.5 Case Studies and Real-Life Examples

Real-life examples illustrate the significant impact of collaborative programs with local churches and organizations.

7.5.1 Food Drive Partnership

Chaplain Lisa partnered with several local churches and a community food bank to organize a large-scale food drive. The collaboration resulted in the collection and distribution of thousands of pounds of food to families in need. The initiative not only provided essential resources but also strengthened community bonds and fostered a sense of solidarity.

7.5.2 Safety Workshop Series

Chaplain Robert collaborated with local organizations to offer a series of safety workshops for the community. Topics included personal safety, emergency preparedness, and cyber security. The workshops were well-attended and received positive feedback, with many participants reporting increased knowledge and confidence in their ability to stay safe.

7.5.3 Grief Support Group

Chaplain Maria partnered with a local church to establish a grief support group for individuals and families dealing with loss. The group met weekly and provided a supportive environment for participants to share their experiences and receive encouragement. Many participants reported significant emotional healing and a renewed sense of hope.

7.6 Essential Qualities for Leading Collaborative Programs

Leading successful collaborative programs requires specific qualities and skills, including:

7.6.1 Compassion

Compassion is essential for understanding and addressing the needs of individuals and the community. Chaplains must demonstrate genuine care and empathy in their interactions.

7.6.2 Leadership

Effective leadership is crucial for organizing and guiding collaborative programs. Chaplains must be able to inspire and motivate others, manage resources, and coordinate activities.

7.6.3 Collaboration

Collaboration is key to successful partnerships. Chaplains must be able to work effectively with a diverse range of partners and stakeholders.

7.6.4 Communication

Effective communication is vital for building relationships, facilitating dialogue, and conveying important information. Chaplains must be able to articulate their thoughts and emotions clearly and empathetically.

7.7 Conclusion

Collaborative programs with local churches and organizations enhance the reach and impact of police chaplaincy programs by providing additional resources and support. These partnerships enable chaplains to extend their services to a broader audience, address diverse needs, and foster a sense of community. By implementing effective strategies and demonstrating essential qualities, chaplains make a significant impact on the well-being of individuals and the strength of community support networks.

CHAPTER 08

ETHICAL AND PROFESSIONAL CHALLENGES

Confidentiality and Trust Issues

Maintaining confidentiality and trust is paramount in police chaplaincy. These elements are foundational to the effectiveness of a chaplain's role, ensuring that officers feel safe to share their deepest concerns and struggles. However, balancing confidentiality with other ethical and professional responsibilities can present significant challenges. This chapter explores these challenges and offers solutions to maintain the integrity of confidentiality and trust within police chaplaincy.

8.1 The Importance of Confidentiality and Trust

Confidentiality and trust are critical for several reasons:

8.1.1 Building Relationships

Trust is the cornerstone of any supportive relationship. Without it, officers are unlikely to open up about their struggles, which limits the chaplain's ability to provide effective support.

8.1.2 Ensuring Safety

Confidentiality ensures that officers feel safe to discuss sensitive issues without fear of repercussions. This safety is crucial for addressing personal and professional challenges that could impact their well-being and job performance.

8.1.3 Promoting Mental Health

A trusted and confidential relationship with a chaplain can encourage officers to seek help early, preventing more severe mental health issues from developing.

8.2 Challenges in Maintaining Confidentiality and Trust

Despite its importance, maintaining confidentiality and trust can be challenging. Some of the primary challenges include:

8.2.1 Legal and Ethical Dilemmas

Chaplains must navigate complex legal and ethical landscapes. There are situations where confidentiality might conflict with legal obligations or the duty to protect the safety of individuals.

- Mandatory Reporting: Chaplains may be required to report certain disclosures, such as threats of harm to oneself or others, which can conflict with the promise of confidentiality.

- Subpoenas and Legal Actions: In some cases, chaplains might be subpoenaed to provide testimony or records, challenging their commitment to confidentiality.

8.2.2 Organizational Pressure

Chaplains may face pressure from police departments or supervisors to disclose information that could be beneficial for administrative or operational purposes.

- Chain of Command: The hierarchical nature of police organizations might lead to requests for information that put chaplains in a difficult position.

- Accountability Measures: There may be expectations for chaplains to provide information for performance reviews or disciplinary actions.

8.2.3 Maintaining Boundaries

Maintaining professional boundaries while building close, trusting relationships can be complex.

- Dual Relationships: Chaplains might find themselves in dual relationships where they are both a confidant and a colleague, complicating the dynamics of confidentiality.

- Emotional Involvement: Deep emotional connections can sometimes blur the lines between professional and personal interactions.

8.3 Strategies for Maintaining Confidentiality and Trust

To navigate these challenges, chaplains can employ various strategies:

8.3.1 Clear Communication

Establishing clear communication about the boundaries and limitations of confidentiality is essential.

- Informed Consent: Clearly explain confidentiality policies and any legal exceptions at the outset of the relationship.

- Regular Reminders: Periodically remind officers about the boundaries of confidentiality to ensure ongoing understanding.

8.3.2 Professional Ethics Training

Ongoing training in professional ethics can help chaplains navigate complex situations.

- Ethical Decision-Making: Training can provide frameworks for making difficult decisions when confidentiality is at stake.

- Legal Knowledge: Understanding relevant laws and regulations helps chaplains anticipate and manage potential conflicts.

8.3.3 Support and Supervision

Access to supervision and peer support can provide chaplains with guidance and a sounding board for difficult situations.

- Regular Supervision: Regular meetings with a supervisor or mentor can provide insights and support for maintaining ethical standards.

- Peer Support Groups: Engaging with other chaplains can offer a space to discuss challenges and share best practices.

8.3.4 Documentation and Record-Keeping

Maintaining accurate and confidential records is crucial.

- Secure Storage: Ensure that all records are stored securely to protect confidentiality.

- Minimal Documentation: Document only what is necessary for the chaplaincy work, avoiding unnecessary details that could compromise confidentiality.

8.4 Balancing Confidentiality with Legal and Ethical Obligations

Balancing confidentiality with legal and ethical obligations requires careful consideration and a structured approach.

8.4.1 Mandatory Reporting

Chaplains must be clear about the circumstances under which they are required to break confidentiality.

- Clear Policies: Develop and communicate clear policies regarding mandatory reporting.

- Prepared Responses: Have prepared responses and protocols for situations that require breaking confidentiality.

8.4.2 Handling Subpoenas and Legal Requests

Developing strategies for handling legal requests for information can help maintain trust.

- Legal Consultation: Consult with legal professionals to understand the best ways to protect confidentiality while complying with legal requirements.

- Resisting Unnecessary Disclosure: Where possible, resist subpoenas and seek to minimize the disclosure of confidential information.

8.5 The Impact of Maintaining Confidentiality and Trust

The diligent maintenance of confidentiality and trust has profound impacts on the effectiveness of police chaplaincy.

8.5.1 Enhanced Trust and Openness

When officers trust that their conversations will remain confidential, they are more likely to seek help and discuss their issues openly.

8.5.2 Better Mental Health Outcomes

Confidential and trusting relationships can lead to early intervention, better coping strategies, and improved mental health outcomes for officers.

8.5.3 Stronger Professional Relationships

Maintaining confidentiality fosters stronger professional relationships, enhancing the overall morale and cohesion within the police force.

8.6 Case Studies and Real-Life Examples

Real-life examples illustrate the challenges and strategies involved in maintaining confidentiality and trust.

8.6.1 Navigating a Mandatory Reporting Situation

Chaplain Sarah faced a situation where an officer disclosed suicidal thoughts. Understanding her mandatory reporting obligations, Sarah explained the limits of confidentiality to the officer, reported the concern to appropriate authorities, and continued to provide support throughout the process.

8.6.2 Handling a Subpoena

Chaplain John received a subpoena for records related to his counseling sessions with an officer involved in a legal case. Consulting with legal counsel, John was able to resist the subpoena and protect the confidentiality of his interactions, reinforcing trust within the department.

8.7 Essential Qualities for Managing Confidentiality and Trust

Managing confidentiality and trust effectively requires specific qualities and skills, including:

8.7.1 Integrity

Integrity is essential for maintaining confidentiality and trust. Chaplains must be steadfast in their ethical commitments and transparent in their actions.

8.7.2 Discretion

Discretion is crucial for handling sensitive information appropriately. Chaplains must be careful about what they share and with whom.

8.7.3 Empathy

Empathy helps chaplains understand the concerns and fears of officers, fostering a trusting relationship.

8.7.4 Ethical Judgment

Sound ethical judgment is necessary for navigating complex situations where confidentiality may be challenged.

8.8 Conclusion

Maintaining confidentiality and trust is paramount in police chaplaincy. While this task presents various challenges, including legal and ethical dilemmas and organizational pressures, effective strategies and a commitment to professional ethics can help chaplains navigate these issues successfully. By ensuring clear communication, continuous training, support, and ethical judgment, chaplains can uphold the integrity of their role and provide meaningful support to law enforcement officers.

This chapter has explored the challenges and solutions related to maintaining confidentiality and trust within police chaplaincy. Subsequent chapters will delve deeper into other aspects of police chaplaincy, including the ongoing professional development and the personal rewards of this essential vocation.

NAVIGATING RELIGIOUS AND SECULAR BOUNDARIES

Introduction

Police chaplains must navigate the complex interplay between religious beliefs and secular responsibilities, ensuring that their support is inclusive and respectful. This balance is essential for maintaining the trust and cooperation of officers and the broader community, which may encompass diverse religious and non-religious backgrounds. This chapter explores the challenges of navigating these boundaries, strategies for maintaining inclusivity, and the impact of effectively managing the intersection of religious and secular roles in police chaplaincy.

8.1 The Importance of Navigating Religious and Secular Boundaries

Understanding and respecting the boundaries between religious beliefs and secular responsibilities is crucial for several reasons:

8.1.1 Inclusivity

Inclusivity ensures that all officers, regardless of their religious or non-religious backgrounds, feel respected and supported.

- Diverse Beliefs: Recognizing and respecting the diverse beliefs within the police force and the community.

- Neutrality: Providing support that is neutral and free from religious bias.

8.1.2 Trust

Maintaining clear boundaries helps build trust between chaplains and those they serve.

- Respect for Personal Beliefs: Demonstrating respect for individual beliefs fosters trust and openness.

- Professionalism: Upholding professional standards that ensure all interactions are respectful and appropriate.

8.1.3 Legal Compliance

Navigating religious and secular boundaries ensures compliance with legal standards and policies.

- Separation of Church and State: Adhering to laws and regulations that mandate the separation of religious activities from government functions.

- Non-Discrimination: Ensuring that all actions comply with non-discrimination policies.

8.2 Challenges in Navigating Religious and Secular Boundaries

Despite its importance, navigating these boundaries can present several challenges:

8.2.1 Diverse Belief Systems

The police force and the community are likely to encompass a wide range of religious and non-religious beliefs.

- Conflicting Beliefs: Managing interactions where personal beliefs may conflict.

- Cultural Sensitivity: Ensuring sensitivity to different cultural and religious practices.

8.2.2 Role Clarity

Chaplains must clearly understand and communicate the distinction between their religious roles and their professional responsibilities.

- Dual Roles: Balancing the dual roles of spiritual advisor and professional support provider.

- Expectation Management: Managing expectations of officers and the community regarding the chaplain's role.

8.2.3 Legal and Ethical Constraints

Chaplains must navigate legal and ethical constraints related to religious activities within a secular institution.

- Religious Neutrality: Ensuring that support provided is neutral and non-coercive.

- Ethical Dilemmas: Addressing ethical dilemmas where religious beliefs may conflict with professional responsibilities.

8.3 Strategies for Maintaining Inclusivity and Respect

Chaplains can employ various strategies to effectively navigate religious and secular boundaries while maintaining inclusivity and respect.

8.3.1 Education and Training

Ongoing education and training are essential for understanding and respecting diverse beliefs.

- Cultural Competency: Training in cultural competency to understand and respect different cultural and religious practices.

- Legal Awareness: Understanding legal requirements and constraints related to religious activities in a secular context.

8.3.2 Clear Communication

Clear communication helps ensure that all interactions are respectful and appropriate.

- Setting Boundaries: Clearly communicating the boundaries of the chaplain's role and the limits of confidentiality.

- Inclusive Language: Using language that is inclusive and respectful of all beliefs.

8.3.3 Collaborative Approach

Collaborating with other professionals and community leaders can enhance the effectiveness of chaplaincy programs.

- Interfaith Partnerships: Partnering with leaders from different faith communities to provide comprehensive support.

- Secular Support Services: Collaborating with secular support services to address diverse needs.

8.4 Providing Inclusive Support

Chaplains must ensure that their support is inclusive and respectful of all beliefs, providing services that are accessible to everyone.

8.4.1 Non-Religious Counseling

Offering non-religious counseling options ensures that all officers feel comfortable seeking support.

- Secular Counseling Techniques: Using counseling techniques that are neutral and non-religious.

- Alternative Support: Providing alternative support options for those who prefer non-religious approaches.

8.4.2 Respecting Individual Beliefs

Respecting the individual beliefs of officers and community members is crucial for building trust and fostering inclusivity.

- Personalized Support: Tailoring support to meet the individual needs and preferences of each person.

- Non-Judgmental Approach: Maintaining a non-judgmental approach to all interactions.

8.5 Balancing Religious and Secular Responsibilities

Balancing religious and secular responsibilities requires careful consideration and structured approaches.

8.5.1 Ethical Decision-Making

Ethical decision-making frameworks can help chaplains navigate complex situations where religious and secular responsibilities intersect.

- Ethical Guidelines: Adhering to ethical guidelines and professional standards.

- Consultation: Seeking consultation and advice when faced with difficult decisions.

8.5.2 Role Clarity

Maintaining clear role definitions helps prevent conflicts and misunderstandings.

- Role Definition: Clearly defining the chaplain's role within the police force.

- Expectation Management: Managing expectations of officers and community members regarding the chaplain's role.

8.6 The Impact of Effectively Navigating Boundaries

Effectively navigating religious and secular boundaries has significant positive impacts on both the police force and the community.

8.6.1 Enhanced Trust and Respect

Respecting diverse beliefs fosters trust and respect between chaplains and those they serve.

- Building Relationships: Stronger relationships based on mutual respect and understanding.

- Fostering Unity: Promoting unity and cooperation within the police force and the community.

8.6.2 Improved Well-Being

Inclusive and respectful support contributes to the overall well-being of officers and community members.

- Mental Health: Improved mental health outcomes through accessible and inclusive support.

- Emotional Support: Enhanced emotional support that respects individual beliefs.

8.6.3 Legal and Ethical Compliance

Ensuring compliance with legal and ethical standards protects the integrity of the chaplaincy program.

- Legal Protection: Avoiding legal issues related to the separation of church and state.

- Ethical Integrity: Upholding ethical standards and maintaining the professional integrity of the chaplaincy role.

8.7 Case Studies and Real-Life Examples

Real-life examples illustrate the challenges and strategies involved in navigating religious and secular boundaries.

8.7.1 Inclusive Memorial Service

Chaplain David organized a memorial service for a fallen officer, ensuring it was inclusive and respectful of all beliefs. By incorporating elements from various religious and non-religious traditions, he provided a meaningful service that honored the officer while respecting the diverse beliefs of attendees.

8.7.2 Ethical Dilemma in Counseling

Chaplain Sarah faced an ethical dilemma when an officer sought her advice on a personal issue that conflicted with her religious beliefs. By focusing on secular counseling techniques and seeking advice from a supervisor, Sarah provided effective support while maintaining professional integrity.

8.8 Essential Qualities for Navigating Religious and Secular Boundaries

Navigating religious and secular boundaries effectively requires specific qualities and skills, including:

8.8.1 Cultural Competency

Cultural competency is essential for understanding and respecting diverse beliefs and practices.

8.8.2 Empathy

Empathy helps chaplains understand the concerns and perspectives of those they serve, fostering inclusive and respectful interactions.

8.8.3 Integrity

Integrity ensures that chaplains uphold ethical standards and maintain professional boundaries.

8.8.4 Communication Skills

Effective communication skills are vital for conveying respect and understanding in all interactions.

8.9 Conclusion

Navigating the complex interplay between religious beliefs and secular responsibilities is a critical aspect of police chaplaincy. By maintaining clear boundaries, demonstrating respect for diverse beliefs, and adhering to ethical and legal standards, chaplains can provide inclusive and effective support. This chapter has explored the challenges and strategies involved in navigating religious and secular boundaries, emphasizing the importance of inclusivity and respect in building trust and fostering well-being within the police force and the community.

Subsequent chapters will delve deeper into other aspects of police chaplaincy, including ongoing professional development and the personal rewards of this essential vocation.

MANAGING PERSONAL FAITH IN A PROFESSIONAL ROLE

Introduction

Balancing personal faith with professional duties requires police chaplains to maintain integrity and objectivity, providing unbiased support to all officers. This balance is essential for fostering trust, respect, and inclusivity within the police force. This chapter explores the challenges chaplains face in managing their personal faith while fulfilling their professional responsibilities, strategies for maintaining objectivity, and the impact of these efforts on the well-being of the officers they serve.

8.1 The Importance of Balancing Personal Faith and Professional Duties

Balancing personal faith with professional duties is crucial for several reasons:

8.1.1 Maintaining Integrity

Maintaining integrity ensures that chaplains remain true to their beliefs while upholding professional standards.

- Consistency: Acting consistently with both personal values and professional ethics.

- Authenticity: Being genuine in interactions with officers and the community.

8.1.2 Ensuring Objectivity

Objectivity is essential for providing unbiased support to all officers, regardless of their personal beliefs.

- Fairness: Treating all officers equally and without prejudice.

- Neutrality: Providing support that is free from personal biases or agendas.

8.1.3 Fostering Trust

Balancing faith and professional duties fosters trust between chaplains and the officers they serve.

- Respect: Demonstrating respect for the diverse beliefs of officers.

- Confidentiality: Ensuring that personal faith does not interfere with maintaining confidentiality and trust.

8.2 Challenges in Managing Personal Faith in a Professional Role

Despite its importance, balancing personal faith with professional duties can present several challenges:

8.2.1 Conflicting Beliefs

Chaplains may encounter situations where their personal beliefs conflict with the needs or beliefs of the officers they serve.

- Ethical Dilemmas: Navigating situations where personal and professional ethics may clash.

- Personal Bias: Ensuring that personal beliefs do not influence professional decisions or support.

8.2.2 Emotional Involvement

Chaplains often develop deep emotional connections with the officers they serve, which can complicate the balance between personal faith and professional responsibilities.

- Empathy and Objectivity: Balancing empathy with the need to remain objective.

- Emotional Boundaries: Maintaining professional boundaries while providing compassionate support.

8.2.3 Role Clarity

Chaplains must clearly understand and communicate the distinction between their personal faith and their professional role.

- Dual Roles: Managing the dual roles of spiritual advisor and professional support provider.

- Expectation Management: Managing the expectations of officers and the community regarding the chaplain's role.

8.3 Strategies for Maintaining Integrity and Objectivity

Chaplains can employ various strategies to effectively balance personal faith with professional duties, maintaining integrity and objectivity in their work.

8.3.1 Professional Development

Ongoing professional development is essential for understanding and addressing the challenges of balancing personal faith and professional duties.

- Ethics Training: Participating in ethics training to develop strategies for navigating ethical dilemmas.

- Cultural Competency: Engaging in cultural competency training to understand and respect diverse beliefs.

8.3.2 Clear Communication

Clear communication helps ensure that all interactions are respectful and appropriate.

- Setting Boundaries: Clearly communicating the boundaries of the chaplain's role and the limits of confidentiality.

- Inclusive Language: Using language that is inclusive and respectful of all beliefs.

8.3.3 Reflective Practice

Reflective practice involves regularly reflecting on one's actions and decisions to ensure they align with both personal values and professional ethics.

- Self-Reflection: Engaging in self-reflection to identify and address any biases or conflicts.

- Supervision and Support: Seeking supervision and support from mentors or peers to discuss and navigate challenging situations.

8.4 Providing Unbiased Support

Chaplains must ensure that their support is unbiased and respectful of all beliefs, providing services that are accessible to everyone.

8.4.1 Non-Religious Counseling

Offering non-religious counseling options ensures that all officers feel comfortable seeking support.

- Secular Counseling Techniques: Using counseling techniques that are neutral and non-religious.

- Alternative Support: Providing alternative support options for those who prefer non-religious approaches.

8.4.2 Respecting Individual Beliefs

Respecting the individual beliefs of officers is crucial for building trust and fostering inclusivity.

- Personalized Support: Tailoring support to meet the individual needs and preferences of each officer.

- Non-Judgmental Approach: Maintaining a non-judgmental approach to all interactions.

8.5 Balancing Personal and Professional Roles

Balancing personal faith and professional duties requires careful consideration and structured approaches.

8.5.1 Ethical Decision-Making

Ethical decision-making frameworks can help chaplains navigate complex situations where personal and professional roles intersect.

- Ethical Guidelines: Adhering to ethical guidelines and professional standards.

- Consultation: Seeking consultation and advice when faced with difficult decisions.

8.5.2 Role Clarity

Maintaining clear role definitions helps prevent conflicts and misunderstandings.

- Role Definition: Clearly defining the chaplain's role within the police force.

- Expectation Management: Managing expectations of officers and community members regarding the chaplain's role.

8.6 The Impact of Managing Personal Faith in a Professional Role

Effectively balancing personal faith with professional duties has significant positive impacts on both the chaplaincy program and the officers it serves.

8.6.1 Enhanced Trust and Respect

Balancing personal faith and professional duties fosters trust and respect between chaplains and officers.

- Building Relationships: Stronger relationships based on mutual respect and understanding.

- Fostering Unity: Promoting unity and cooperation within the police force.

8.6.2 Improved Well-Being

Inclusive and unbiased support contributes to the overall well-being of officers.

- Mental Health: Improved mental health outcomes through accessible and inclusive support.

- Emotional Support: Enhanced emotional support that respects individual beliefs.

8.6.3 Professional Integrity

Maintaining integrity and objectivity upholds the professional standards of the chaplaincy program.

- Ethical Standards: Ensuring adherence to ethical standards and professional guidelines.

- Program Credibility: Enhancing the credibility and trustworthiness of the chaplaincy program.

8.7 Case Studies and Real-Life Examples

Real-life examples illustrate the challenges and strategies involved in managing personal faith in a professional role.

8.7.1 Navigating an Ethical Dilemma

Chaplain Emily faced an ethical dilemma when an officer sought her advice on a personal issue that conflicted with her religious beliefs. By focusing on secular counseling techniques and seeking advice from a supervisor, Emily provided effective support while maintaining professional integrity.

8.7.2 Providing Inclusive Support

Chaplain Michael developed a counseling program that offered both religious and non-religious support options. This inclusive approach ensured that all officers felt respected and comfortable seeking help, regardless of their personal beliefs.

8.8 Essential Qualities for Balancing Personal Faith and Professional Duties

Balancing personal faith with professional duties effectively requires specific qualities and skills, including:

8.8.1 Integrity

Integrity is essential for maintaining consistency between personal values and professional ethics.

8.8.2 Objectivity

Objectivity ensures that chaplains provide unbiased support to all officers.

8.8.3 Empathy

Empathy helps chaplains understand and respect the diverse beliefs and needs of officers.

8.8.4 Communication Skills

Effective communication skills are vital for conveying respect and understanding in all interactions.

8.9 Conclusion

Managing personal faith in a professional role is a critical aspect of police chaplaincy. By maintaining integrity and objectivity, chaplains can provide unbiased support that respects the diverse beliefs of officers. This chapter has explored the challenges and strategies involved in balancing personal faith with professional duties, emphasizing the importance of inclusivity and respect in fostering trust and well-being within the police force.

Subsequent chapters will delve deeper into other aspects of police chaplaincy, including ongoing professional development and the personal rewards of this essential vocation.

CHAPTER 09

CASE STUDIES AND STORIES

Real-Life Experiences from the Field

Real-life experiences of police chaplains illustrate the profound impact of their work on the officers and communities they serve. These stories highlight the challenges, triumphs, and everyday realities of chaplaincy, providing valuable insights into the essential role chaplains play within law enforcement. This chapter presents a series of case studies and personal stories that demonstrate the significant contributions and diverse responsibilities of police chaplains.

9.1 Case Study: Supporting an Officer Through Grief

Background

Officer James had been with the police force for over a decade when his partner was killed in the line of duty. The tragic loss left James devastated, struggling with grief and questioning his ability to continue his work.

Intervention

Chaplain Sarah reached out to James immediately following the incident, offering her support and presence. She provided grief counseling, helping James process his emotions and come to terms with the loss. Sarah also facilitated support group meetings with other officers who had experienced similar losses, creating a space for shared experiences and mutual support.

Outcome

Through consistent counseling and the support group, James gradually began to heal. He found solace in sharing his grief with colleagues and developed coping strategies to manage his emotions. Sarah's compassionate support and the community she fostered were instrumental in helping James navigate this challenging period, ultimately allowing him to continue his service with renewed strength and resilience.

9.2 Case Study: Crisis Intervention During a Hostage Situation

Background

A tense hostage situation unfolded at a local bank, involving multiple hostages and an armed suspect. The situation required a coordinated response from law enforcement, including the SWAT team and crisis negotiators.

Intervention

Chaplain Mark was called to the scene to provide support to the officers involved. He offered immediate emotional support to the negotiators, helping them manage the stress and maintain their focus. Mark also stayed with the officers on standby, providing a calming presence and offering prayers for safety and a peaceful resolution.

Outcome

The hostage situation was resolved without any casualties, thanks in part to the composed efforts of the negotiators and the SWAT team. The officers expressed gratitude for Mark's presence, noting that his support helped them stay grounded and focused during the crisis. Mark's involvement highlighted the critical role chaplains play in high-stress situations, offering essential emotional and spiritual support.

9.3 Case Study: Organizing a Community Outreach Event

Background

In response to growing tensions between law enforcement and the community, Chaplain Maria organized a community outreach event aimed at fostering positive relationships and open dialogue.

Intervention

Maria collaborated with local churches, community organizations, and police departments to plan the event. The outreach included activities such as a community barbecue, safety demonstrations, and informational booths. Maria also facilitated a town hall meeting where community members could voice their concerns and engage in constructive conversations with law enforcement officers.

Outcome

The event was a resounding success, attracting hundreds of community members and officers. The barbecue and activities provided a relaxed setting for positive interactions, while the town hall meeting allowed for meaningful dialogue and understanding. Many attendees expressed appreciation for the opportunity to connect with law enforcement in a non-confrontational environment. Maria's initiative helped to bridge gaps, build trust, and promote a sense of unity within the community.

9.4 Story: Providing Support During Personal Crisis

Background

Officer Lisa, a single mother, was struggling to balance her demanding job with her responsibilities at home. The stress of managing her career and family life was taking a toll on her mental health.

Intervention

Chaplain John noticed the signs of stress and reached out to Lisa. He offered her a listening ear and provided counseling to help her navigate her challenges. John also connected Lisa with community resources, including a support group for single parents and a local charity that offered childcare assistance.

Outcome

With John's support, Lisa was able to find a better balance between her work and home life. The counseling sessions helped her develop coping strategies, and the community resources provided much-needed relief. Lisa's improved well-being positively impacted her performance at work and her relationships with her children. John's proactive and compassionate approach exemplified the vital role chaplains play in supporting officers' overall well-being.

9.5 Story: Interfaith Collaboration for Inclusive Support

Background

The police department served a diverse community with multiple religious backgrounds. Chaplain David recognized the need for an inclusive approach to chaplaincy that respected and accommodated various faiths.

Intervention

David initiated an interfaith collaboration, bringing together leaders from different religious communities to discuss how they could collectively support the police force and the community. He organized interfaith prayer services, cultural competence training for officers, and joint community service projects.

Outcome

The interfaith collaboration fostered a greater understanding and respect for different religious traditions within the police force and the community. Officers became more culturally competent, improving their interactions with diverse community members. The joint service projects built stronger relationships between the police and the community, enhancing trust and cooperation. David's efforts demonstrated the importance of inclusivity and respect in chaplaincy work.

9.6 Case Study: Supporting Mental Health Initiatives

Background

Recognizing the increasing mental health challenges faced by officers, Chaplain Emily advocated for the implementation of comprehensive mental health initiatives within the department.

Intervention

Emily collaborated with mental health professionals to develop a mental health program that included regular counseling sessions, stress management workshops, and peer support groups. She also facilitated training sessions for officers on recognizing and addressing mental health issues.

Outcome

The mental health program led to a significant improvement in the overall well-being of the officers. The counseling sessions and workshops provided valuable tools for managing stress, while the peer support groups fostered a sense of community and mutual support. Officers reported feeling more equipped to handle the demands of their job, and the stigma surrounding mental health began to diminish. Emily's advocacy and dedication to mental health highlighted the critical role of chaplains in promoting psychological well-being.

9.7 Story: Facilitating Healing After a Traumatic Incident

Background

A traumatic incident involving a mass casualty event deeply affected the entire police force. The officers involved were struggling with intense emotions and symptoms of PTSD.

Intervention

Chaplain Robert organized a series of debriefing sessions and trauma-focused counseling for the affected officers. He also brought in trauma specialists to provide additional support and conducted spiritual healing services for those who desired it.

Outcome

The debriefing sessions and counseling helped the officers process their experiences and begin their healing journey. The spiritual services provided comfort and a sense of closure for many. The comprehensive support Robert facilitated played a crucial role in the officers' recovery, demonstrating the multifaceted approach needed to address trauma effectively.

9.8 Conclusion

These case studies and stories illustrate the profound impact police chaplains have on the officers and communities they serve. Through their compassionate support, proactive initiatives, and inclusive approaches, chaplains address a wide range of needs and challenges within law enforcement. Their work fosters trust, promotes well-being, and strengthens the bonds between the police force and the community. These real-life experiences underscore the essential role of chaplains in maintaining the mental, emotional, and spiritual health of those who serve and protect.

In the following chapters, we will delve deeper into the ongoing professional development required for effective chaplaincy and the personal rewards that come from serving in this vital role.

IMPACTFUL MOMENTS AND LESSONS LEARNED

Introduction

Throughout their careers, police chaplains encounter numerous impactful moments that shape their approach to ministry and support within law enforcement. These experiences offer valuable lessons and insights, providing inspiration and guidance for future chaplains. This chapter presents a collection of significant moments and lessons learned, highlighting the profound impact chaplains have on the officers and communities they serve.

9.1 Impactful Moments in Chaplaincy

9.1.1 The Power of Presence

Chaplain Sarah recalls a time when her mere presence made a significant difference during a critical incident.

- Moment: Sarah was called to the scene of a severe traffic accident involving an officer. While medical teams worked, Sarah stood by the officer's side, offering silent support and prayers.

- Lesson Learned: The power of presence cannot be underestimated. Sometimes, just being there provides immense comfort and reassurance.

9.1.2 Bridging Gaps During a Crisis

Chaplain Mark shares an experience where he acted as a bridge between officers and the community during a tense standoff.

- Moment: During a standoff, tensions were high between the police and the local community. Mark facilitated communication between both parties, helping to de-escalate the situation.

- Lesson Learned: Effective communication and mediation are crucial skills for chaplains. Building trust with both officers and the community can prevent escalation and promote understanding.

9.1.3 Providing Hope in Dark Times

Chaplain Maria reflects on a moment when she provided hope to an officer struggling with depression.

- Moment: An officer confided in Maria about his severe depression and suicidal thoughts. Through consistent counseling and support, Maria helped him find hope and seek professional help.

- Lesson Learned: Offering hope and being a consistent source of support can save lives. Chaplains must be vigilant and proactive in recognizing signs of mental health struggles.

9.2 Lessons Learned from the Field

9.2.1 The Importance of Self-Care

Chaplain Emily emphasizes the necessity of self-care for chaplains to avoid burnout.

- Lesson Learned: Self-care is essential for maintaining one's ability to provide support. Chaplains must prioritize their mental, emotional, and physical health to continue serving effectively.

9.2.2 Adaptability in Diverse Situations

Chaplain John highlights the need for adaptability in various situations encountered in police chaplaincy.

- Lesson Learned: Flexibility and adaptability are key. Chaplains must be prepared to handle a wide range of scenarios, from critical incidents to everyday support, and adjust their approach accordingly.

9.2.3 Continuous Learning and Development

Chaplain David underscores the importance of ongoing learning and professional development.

- Lesson Learned: Continuous learning is vital for staying effective and relevant. Engaging in ongoing training, seeking new knowledge, and learning from each experience enhance a chaplain's ability to serve.

9.3 Inspirational Stories

9.3.1 Transforming Lives Through Faith

Chaplain Robert shares an inspirational story about helping an officer rediscover his faith.

- Story: An officer who had lost his faith after experiencing trauma found spiritual renewal through Robert's guidance. This transformation not only improved the officer's mental health but also reinvigorated his commitment to serving the community.

- Inspiration: Faith can be a powerful tool for healing and transformation. Chaplains have the opportunity to guide individuals on their spiritual journeys, leading to profound personal growth.

9.3.2 Strengthening Community Bonds

Chaplain Lisa recounts a successful initiative that strengthened community bonds through collaborative efforts.

- Story: Lisa organized a series of community service projects involving officers and local residents. These projects fostered a sense of unity and mutual respect, improving the relationship between the police force and the community.

- Inspiration: Community engagement and collaboration can bridge divides and build stronger, more resilient communities. Chaplains play a crucial role in facilitating these connections.

9.3.3 Overcoming Personal Adversity

Chaplain Michael reflects on his journey of overcoming personal adversity and how it shaped his approach to chaplaincy.

- Story: Michael faced significant personal challenges, including loss and health issues. These experiences deepened his empathy and understanding, enhancing his ability to connect with and support officers facing their struggles.

- Inspiration: Personal adversity can be a source of strength and wisdom. Chaplains who have overcome their challenges often bring a unique and valuable perspective to their work.

9.4 Practical Advice for Future Chaplains

9.4.1 Building Trust

Chaplain Sarah advises future chaplains on the importance of building trust with officers.

- Advice: Trust is the foundation of effective chaplaincy. Be consistent, honest, and respectful in all interactions. Building trust takes time but is essential for providing meaningful support.

9.4.2 Embracing Diversity

Chaplain Mark encourages future chaplains to embrace diversity within the police force and the community.

- Advice: Embrace and respect the diverse backgrounds and beliefs of those you serve. Cultural competency and inclusivity are critical for effective chaplaincy.

9.4.3 Staying Grounded

Chaplain Maria offers advice on staying grounded and maintaining a strong sense of purpose.

- Advice: Stay connected to your values and the reasons you became a chaplain. Reflect regularly on your experiences and seek support when needed to stay grounded and focused.

9.5 Conclusion

The experiences and lessons shared by police chaplains highlight the profound impact of their work on the officers and communities they serve. These stories and insights provide valuable guidance and inspiration for future chaplains, emphasizing the importance of trust, inclusivity, adaptability, and continuous learning. The role of a chaplain is both challenging and rewarding, offering unique opportunities to support and transform lives.

As we look ahead, these lessons and experiences serve as a testament to the vital role chaplains play within law enforcement, reminding us of the importance of compassion, integrity, and dedication in this essential vocation. Subsequent chapters will delve deeper into ongoing professional development and the personal rewards that come from serving as a police chaplain.

TESTIMONIALS FROM OFFICERS AND THEIR FAMILIES

Introduction

Testimonials from officers and their families provide a powerful testament to the value and importance of police chaplaincy. These personal accounts highlight the profound impact that chaplains have on the well-being and resilience of law enforcement personnel and their loved ones. This chapter presents a collection of heartfelt testimonials that underscore the critical role chaplains play in supporting the mental, emotional, and spiritual health of those they serve.

9.1 Testimonials from Officers

9.1.1 Officer James: Finding Hope in Dark Times

"I was at my lowest point, struggling with depression and feeling completely overwhelmed by the demands of the job. Chaplain Sarah reached out to me when I needed it most.

Her compassion and unwavering support gave me the strength to seek professional help and start my journey to recovery. I truly believe that without her intervention, I wouldn't be here today. Chaplaincy is not just a job for Sarah; it's her calling, and it makes all the difference."

9.1.2 Officer Maria: A Beacon of Support

"After a particularly traumatic incident, I found it difficult to cope with the emotional aftermath. Chaplain Mark was there every step of the way, providing a safe space to talk about my feelings and offering practical advice to manage my stress. His presence and guidance were instrumental in helping me regain my confidence and resilience. Mark's dedication to the well-being of officers is evident in everything he does, and I am incredibly grateful for his support."

9.1.3 Officer David: Bridging the Gap

"Community relations were strained, and tensions were high. Chaplain Lisa organized a community outreach event that brought officers and residents together in a positive, constructive environment. Her ability to bridge the gap between law enforcement and the community was remarkable. The event fostered understanding and mutual respect, and it wouldn't have been possible without Lisa's vision and leadership. She has a unique gift for bringing people together."

9.2 Testimonials from Families

9.2.1 Emily: A Spouse's Gratitude

"My husband, Officer John, was dealing with immense stress from his job, and it was affecting our family life. Chaplain Emily reached out to us and offered not only support for John but also resources for our entire family. She provided counseling sessions, connected us with support groups, and checked in regularly. Emily's support has been a lifeline for our family, helping us navigate through challenging times and strengthening our bond."

9.2.2 The Rodriguez Family: Healing After Loss

"When we lost my brother, Officer Alex, in the line of duty, our world was shattered. Chaplain Robert was there for us from the moment we received the devastating news. He guided us through the funeral arrangements, provided grief counseling, and offered ongoing support. Robert's kindness and compassion helped us begin the healing process. He made us feel like we weren't alone in our grief, and for that, we will always be grateful."

9.2.3 Sarah: A Mother's Perspective

"My son, Officer Michael, was involved in a critical incident that left him traumatized. Chaplain David provided the emotional and spiritual support Michael needed to start his recovery. David also supported us, his family, by helping us understand what Michael was going through and how we could best support him. The chaplaincy program has been invaluable to our family, providing comfort and hope during a very difficult time."

9.3 Testimonials Highlighting Specific Chaplaincy Programs

9.3.1 Peer Support Program

"Chaplain John initiated a peer support program that has been a game-changer for our department. It allows us to support each other in ways we couldn't before. Having trained peers who understand what we're going through has made a huge difference in our mental health and morale. John's leadership and commitment to our well-being have transformed the culture within our department."

9.3.2 Stress Management Workshops

"Chaplain Maria's stress management workshops have equipped us with practical tools to handle the daily pressures of the job. Her workshops are interactive and engaging, providing valuable strategies that we can apply both on and off duty. Maria's approachability and expertise make her workshops a must-attend for any officer looking to improve their mental health and resilience."

9.3.3 Family Support Services

"Chaplain Sarah's family support services have been a blessing for our family. The counseling sessions and resources she provides have helped us navigate the unique challenges of having a loved one in law enforcement. Sarah's dedication to supporting not just the officers but also their families has strengthened our family unit and improved our overall well-being. We are incredibly grateful for her compassion and support."

9.4 Testimonials from Community Members

9.4.1 Building Trust and Understanding

"As a community leader, I have seen firsthand the positive impact Chaplain Mark's initiatives have had on our neighborhood. His efforts to foster dialogue and understanding between law enforcement and residents have built bridges of trust and cooperation. Mark's commitment to inclusivity and respect has transformed our relationship with the police, making our community safer and more connected."

9.4.2 Youth Mentorship Program

"Chaplain Emily's youth mentorship program has been a lifeline for many at-risk youth in our community. By pairing them with positive role models from the police force, she has provided guidance, support, and hope for a better future. Emily's dedication to our youth has not only changed lives but also strengthened the bond between our community and law enforcement."

9.4.3 Interfaith Collaboration

"Chaplain David's interfaith collaboration initiatives have brought together leaders from various religious communities to work towards common goals. His ability to foster unity and cooperation among diverse groups has been inspiring. David's inclusive approach has not only enriched our community but also demonstrated the power of faith and collaboration in addressing shared challenges."

9.5 Conclusion

The testimonials from officers, their families, and community members provide a powerful testament to the value and importance of police chaplaincy. These personal accounts highlight the profound impact that chaplains have on the well-being and resilience of law enforcement personnel and their loved ones. The support, compassion, and leadership provided by chaplains are invaluable, fostering trust, promoting mental health, and building stronger communities.

As we reflect on these testimonials, it is clear that the role of a police chaplain is both challenging and immensely rewarding. The dedication and commitment of chaplains to serving those who protect and serve are a testament to the essential nature of their work. Subsequent chapters will delve deeper into ongoing professional development and the personal rewards that come from serving as a police chaplain.

CHAPTER 10

CRISIS AND DISASTER RESPONSE

Role in Major Incidents and Disasters

Police chaplains play a vital role in responding to major incidents and disasters, providing essential support and guidance during these challenging times. Their presence and actions can make a significant difference in the lives of officers, victims, and communities affected by crises. This chapter explores the various roles and responsibilities of police chaplains during major incidents and disasters, highlighting their contributions and the strategies they use to provide effective support.

10.1 The Importance of Chaplaincy in Crisis and Disaster Response

10.1.1 Emotional and Spiritual Support

Chaplains provide emotional and spiritual support to those affected by major incidents and disasters.

- Comfort and Reassurance: Offering comfort and reassurance to individuals experiencing shock, fear, and grief.

- Spiritual Guidance: Providing spiritual support and guidance tailored to the individual's beliefs and needs.

10.1.2 Crisis Intervention

Chaplains play a critical role in crisis intervention, helping to stabilize situations and provide immediate support.

- On-Scene Presence: Being present at the scene of incidents to offer immediate support and comfort.

- Psychological First Aid: Providing psychological first aid to help individuals manage their immediate emotional and psychological responses.

10.1.3 Coordination and Communication

Chaplains often serve as liaisons between law enforcement, victims, and community resources, facilitating effective communication and coordination.

- Resource Connection: Connecting individuals with necessary resources and support services.

- Information Dissemination: Helping to disseminate accurate and timely information to affected individuals and communities.

10.2 Roles and Responsibilities During Major Incidents

10.2.1 Immediate Response

Chaplains are often among the first responders during major incidents, providing critical support in the immediate aftermath.

- Support for First Responders: Offering emotional support and practical assistance to first responders, helping them cope with the stress and demands of the situation.

- Victim Assistance: Providing immediate support to victims, helping them navigate the initial shock and trauma.

10.2.2 Ongoing Support and Counseling

Beyond the immediate response, chaplains provide ongoing support and counseling to those affected by major incidents.

- Follow-Up Care: Ensuring ongoing emotional and psychological support for first responders, victims, and their families.

- Grief Counseling: Offering grief counseling and support to individuals and families dealing with loss.

10.2.3 Memorial Services and Ceremonies

Chaplains often organize and conduct memorial services and ceremonies to honor those affected by major incidents.

- Planning and Coordination: Coordinating with families, law enforcement, and community leaders to plan meaningful services.

- Conducting Services: Leading memorial services and ceremonies that provide comfort and closure for those in mourning.

10.3 Strategies for Effective Crisis and Disaster Response

10.3.1 Training and Preparation

Effective crisis response requires thorough training and preparation.

- Crisis Intervention Training: Participating in specialized training programs to develop skills in crisis intervention and psychological first aid.

- Scenario-Based Training: Engaging in scenario-based training exercises to simulate real-life incidents and improve response capabilities.

10.3.2 Building Relationships and Networks

Building strong relationships and networks is crucial for effective crisis response.

- Interagency Collaboration: Collaborating with other agencies and organizations to ensure a coordinated response.

- Community Engagement: Building relationships with community leaders and organizations to facilitate effective communication and support during crises.

10.3.3 Self-Care and Resilience

Chaplains must prioritize their own self-care and resilience to maintain their effectiveness during crises.

- Regular Self-Care Practices: Engaging in regular self-care practices to manage stress and prevent burnout.

- Peer Support: Seeking support from peers and supervisors to process experiences and maintain emotional well-being.

10.4 Case Studies and Real-Life Examples

10.4.1 Natural Disaster Response

Chaplain Sarah's role during a major hurricane response highlights the importance of chaplaincy in disaster situations.

- Immediate Support: Sarah provided immediate emotional support to first responders and victims, helping them manage their shock and fear.

- Ongoing Counseling: She offered ongoing counseling to those affected, helping them process their trauma and begin the recovery process.

- Community Coordination: Sarah coordinated with local organizations to ensure that victims received necessary resources and support.

10.4.2 Mass Casualty Incident

Chaplain Mark's involvement in a mass casualty incident underscores the critical role of chaplains in providing support during major crises.

- On-Scene Presence: Mark was present at the scene, offering comfort and reassurance to first responders and victims.

- Memorial Services: He organized and conducted memorial services for the victims, providing a space for the community to grieve and find closure.

- Follow-Up Care: Mark provided ongoing support and counseling to first responders, helping them cope with the emotional aftermath of the incident.

10.5 Essential Qualities for Crisis and Disaster Response

Effective crisis and disaster response requires specific qualities and skills, including:

10.5.1 Compassion

Compassion is essential for providing emotional and spiritual support during crises.

10.5.2 Resilience

Resilience helps chaplains manage the emotional toll of their work and maintain their effectiveness.

10.5.3 Communication Skills

Effective communication skills are vital for coordinating with other responders and providing clear, comforting guidance to those affected.

10.5.4 Flexibility

Flexibility is important for adapting to rapidly changing situations and addressing diverse needs during crises.

10.6 Conclusion

Police chaplains play a vital role in responding to major incidents and disasters, offering essential support and guidance during these challenging times. Through their presence, compassion, and expertise, chaplains provide critical emotional and spiritual support to first responders, victims, and communities. Their contributions help stabilize situations, facilitate recovery, and foster resilience in the face of adversity.

This chapter has explored the various roles and responsibilities of police chaplains during major incidents and disasters, highlighting their impact and the strategies they use to provide effective support. The following chapters will delve into other aspects of police chaplaincy, including ongoing professional development and the personal rewards of serving in this essential role.

SUPPORT GRIEVING FAMILIES AND COLLEAGUES

Introduction

Providing comfort and care to grieving families and colleagues is a core responsibility of police chaplains. This essential support helps individuals navigate the aftermath of loss, offering emotional and spiritual guidance during one of the most challenging times in their lives. This chapter explores the role of police chaplains in supporting grieving families and colleagues, the strategies they employ, and the profound impact of their compassionate care.

10.1 The Importance of Supporting Grieving Families and Colleagues

10.1.1 Emotional Stability

Grieving can be an overwhelming experience, and the support of a chaplain can help provide emotional stability.

- Listening Ear: Offering a compassionate presence and a listening ear to those in grief.

- Emotional Validation: Acknowledging and validating the feelings of the bereaved, helping them feel understood and supported.

10.1.2 Spiritual Comfort

Chaplains provide spiritual comfort that aligns with the beliefs and needs of grieving individuals.

- Spiritual Guidance: Providing prayers, religious rituals, or spiritual conversations that offer solace.

- Faith-Based Support: Drawing on religious or spiritual beliefs to provide hope and meaning during difficult times.

10.1.3 Practical Assistance

In addition to emotional and spiritual support, chaplains can offer practical assistance to grieving families and colleagues.

- Funeral Planning: Assisting with funeral arrangements and memorial services.

- Resource Connection: Connecting families with grief counseling, support groups, and other resources.

10.2 Roles and Responsibilities in Grief Support

10.2.1 Immediate Response

Chaplains often provide immediate support following the news of a death.

- Notification Support: Accompanying officers who deliver death notifications to families.

- On-Scene Support: Providing comfort to colleagues and family members at the scene of a fatal incident.

10.2.2 Ongoing Counseling and Support

Ongoing support is crucial for helping individuals process their grief and begin healing.

- Grief Counseling: Offering individual and group counseling sessions to help the bereaved navigate their emotions.

- Regular Check-Ins: Maintaining regular contact with grieving families and colleagues to provide continuous support.

10.2.3 Memorial Services and Ceremonies

Chaplains play a key role in planning and conducting memorial services and ceremonies.

- Service Planning: Coordinating with families and colleagues to plan meaningful services that honor the deceased.

- Conducting Services: Leading memorial services and providing spiritual guidance during these ceremonies.

10.3 Strategies for Effective Grief Support

10.3.1 Active Listening and Presence

Active listening and being fully present are fundamental strategies in providing effective grief support.

- Attentive Listening: Listening without interruption, allowing the bereaved to express their feelings and stories.

- Non-Verbal Support: Offering a comforting presence through non-verbal cues like eye contact and gentle touch.

10.3.2 Personalized Support

Providing personalized support ensures that the needs and preferences of grieving individuals are met.

- Tailored Approach: Adapting support to align with the cultural, religious, and personal preferences of the bereaved.

- Individual Focus: Recognizing that grief is unique to each person and responding accordingly.

10.3.3 Collaboration with Other Professionals

Collaborating with other professionals enhances the support provided to grieving families and colleagues.

- Mental Health Professionals: Working with counselors and therapists to provide comprehensive emotional support.

- Community Resources: Connecting families with community resources such as support groups and financial assistance programs.

10.4 Case Studies and Real-Life Examples

10.4.1 Supporting a Family After a Line-of-Duty Death

Chaplain Sarah's role in supporting a family after a line-of-duty death illustrates the importance of immediate and ongoing support.

- Immediate Response: Sarah was present when the family was notified, offering immediate comfort and support.

- Funeral Planning: She assisted with the funeral arrangements, ensuring that the service honored the officer's life and service.

- Ongoing Support: Sarah maintained regular contact with the family, providing continuous emotional and spiritual support.

10.4.2 Helping Colleagues Cope with Loss

Chaplain Mark's support for a police department after the sudden death of a beloved colleague highlights the role of chaplains in workplace grief.

- On-Scene Support: Mark was present at the station, offering support to officers as they processed the news.

- Grief Counseling: He organized group counseling sessions to help officers express their grief and support one another.

- Memorial Service: Mark planned and conducted a memorial service at the station, providing a space for colleagues to mourn and honor their friend.

10.5 Essential Qualities for Supporting Grieving Individuals

Supporting grieving families and colleagues requires specific qualities and skills, including:

10.5.1 Empathy

Empathy is crucial for understanding and connecting with those who are grieving.

- Understanding Feelings: Demonstrating genuine care and understanding for the emotions of the bereaved.

- Emotional Support: Offering compassionate and non-judgmental support.

10.5.2 Patience

Grieving is a process that takes time, and patience is essential for providing ongoing support.

- Allowing Time: Giving individuals the time they need to process their grief without pressure.

- Consistent Presence: Being a steady and reliable source of support throughout the grieving process.

10.5.3 Communication Skills

Effective communication is vital for providing clear, comforting guidance to grieving individuals.

- Clear Communication: Providing information and support in a clear and sensitive manner.

- Active Listening: Ensuring that the bereaved feel heard and understood.

10.6 Conclusion

Providing comfort and care to grieving families and colleagues is a core responsibility of police chaplains. Through their compassionate presence, spiritual guidance, and practical assistance, chaplains help individuals navigate the aftermath of loss and begin the healing process. The support offered by chaplains is invaluable, fostering emotional stability, spiritual comfort, and a sense of community during times of profound grief.

This chapter has explored the roles and responsibilities of police chaplains in supporting grieving families and colleagues, highlighting the strategies they use and the impact of their compassionate care. The following chapters will delve into other aspects of police chaplaincy, including ongoing professional development and the personal rewards of serving in this essential role.

LONG-TERM IMPACT AND FOLLOW-UP CARE

Introduction

Chaplains provide ongoing support and follow-up care to ensure that the emotional and psychological needs of officers and their families are met in the long term. This commitment to continued care is crucial for fostering resilience, promoting healing, and maintaining well-being long after the initial crisis or loss. This chapter explores the importance of long-term impact and follow-up care in police chaplaincy, the strategies chaplains use, and the profound effects of sustained support.

10.1 The Importance of Long-Term Support and Follow-Up Care

10.1.1 Promoting Healing and Recovery

Long-term support is essential for promoting healing and recovery after traumatic events or losses.

- Continued Counseling: Providing ongoing counseling helps individuals process their experiences and emotions over time.

- Support Systems: Ensuring that individuals have access to robust support systems to aid in their recovery.

10.1.2 Preventing Isolation

Follow-up care helps prevent individuals from feeling isolated in their grief or trauma.

- Regular Check-Ins: Maintaining regular contact to offer support and show that they are not alone.

- Community Integration: Encouraging participation in community and support group activities.

10.1.3 Building Resilience

Sustained support helps build resilience, enabling individuals to cope better with future challenges.

- Resilience Training: Providing tools and strategies to enhance emotional and psychological resilience.

- Empowerment: Empowering individuals to take proactive steps in their healing journey.

10.2 Roles and Responsibilities in Long-Term Care

10.2.1 Ongoing Counseling and Support

Chaplains offer ongoing counseling and support to help individuals continue their healing process.

- Individual Counseling: Providing personalized counseling sessions tailored to the needs of each individual.

- Group Support: Facilitating support groups where individuals can share experiences and support each other.

10.2.2 Regular Check-Ins and Follow-Ups

Maintaining regular check-ins ensures that individuals receive continuous support.

- Scheduled Follow-Ups: Setting up regular follow-up appointments to monitor progress and address any emerging issues.

- Ad Hoc Support: Being available for additional support as needed.

10.2.3 Community and Resource Connection

Connecting individuals with community resources and support networks is a vital part of long-term care.

- Resource Referrals: Referring individuals to additional resources such as mental health professionals, support groups, and community services.

- Building Networks: Helping individuals build strong support networks within their community.

10.3 Strategies for Effective Long-Term Impact and Follow-Up Care

10.3.1 Personalized Care Plans

Developing personalized care plans ensures that the support provided meets the unique needs of each individual.

- Assessment: Conducting thorough assessments to understand the specific needs and challenges of each individual.

- Tailored Interventions: Designing interventions and support strategies that are personalized and relevant.

10.3.2 Building Trust and Rapport

Building and maintaining trust is essential for effective long-term care.

- Consistent Support: Providing reliable and consistent support to build trust.

- Open Communication: Encouraging open and honest communication to foster a strong therapeutic relationship.

10.3.3 Collaboration with Other Professionals

Collaborating with other professionals enhances the effectiveness of long-term care.

- Multi-Disciplinary Approach: Working with mental health professionals, social workers, and other relevant professionals to provide comprehensive support.

- Coordinated Care: Ensuring that all aspects of an individual's care are well-coordinated and integrated.

10.4 Case Studies and Real-Life Examples

10.4.1 Long-Term Support After a Traumatic Incident

Chaplain Sarah's role in providing long-term support to an officer after a traumatic incident illustrates the importance of sustained care.

- Initial Support: Sarah provided immediate emotional support following the incident.

- Ongoing Counseling: She continued to offer regular counseling sessions to help the officer process the trauma.

- Building Resilience: Sarah introduced resilience training to help the officer develop coping strategies for future challenges.

10.4.2 Follow-Up Care for Grieving Families

Chaplain Mark's commitment to follow-up care for a grieving family highlights the impact of long-term support.

- Initial Response: Mark provided immediate support to the family after the loss of a loved one in the line of duty.

- Regular Check-Ins: He maintained regular contact with the family, offering continuous emotional and spiritual support.

- Community Connection: Mark connected the family with local support groups and resources to help them integrate into a supportive community network.

10.5 Essential Qualities for Providing Long-Term Care

Providing effective long-term care requires specific qualities and skills, including:

10.5.1 Empathy

Empathy is crucial for understanding and connecting with individuals on a deep emotional level.

- Genuine Care: Demonstrating genuine concern and care for the well-being of individuals.

- Emotional Support: Offering compassionate and non-judgmental support.

10.5.2 Patience

Patience is essential for providing ongoing support over an extended period.

- Allowing Time: Giving individuals the time they need to heal and recover.

- Consistent Presence: Being a steady and reliable source of support throughout the healing process.

10.5.3 Communication Skills

Effective communication skills are vital for providing clear, comforting guidance and maintaining open dialogue.

- Active Listening: Ensuring that individuals feel heard and understood.

- Clear Guidance: Providing information and support in a clear and sensitive manner.

10.6 The Impact of Long-Term Care

The impact of long-term care provided by chaplains is profound and far-reaching.

10.6.1 Enhanced Well-Being

Ongoing support contributes significantly to the overall well-being of individuals.

- Mental Health: Improved mental health outcomes through sustained support and counseling.

- Emotional Stability: Greater emotional stability and resilience.

10.6.2 Stronger Relationships

Long-term care helps strengthen relationships between individuals and their support networks.

- Family Bonds: Enhanced family relationships through continuous support and guidance.

- Community Integration: Stronger integration into community support networks.

10.6.3 Increased Resilience

Sustained support helps build resilience, enabling individuals to cope better with future challenges.

- Coping Strategies: Improved coping strategies and emotional resilience.

- Empowerment: Empowerment to take proactive steps in their healing journey.

10.7 Conclusion

Chaplains provide ongoing support and follow-up care to ensure that the emotional and psychological needs of officers and their families are met in the long term. Through continued counseling, regular check-ins, and community connection, chaplains foster healing, resilience, and well-being. Their commitment to long-term care has a profound impact, helping individuals navigate the aftermath of trauma and loss, and promoting sustained recovery and growth.

CHAPTER 11

INTERFAITH AND MULTICULTURAL DYNAMICS

Respecting Diverse Beliefs

Police chaplains must respect and accommodate diverse religious beliefs within the force, promoting inclusivity and understanding. This chapter explores the challenges and strategies associated with navigating interfaith and multicultural dynamics, highlighting the importance of respect, empathy, and cultural competence in fostering a cohesive and supportive environment.

11.1 The Importance of Respecting Diverse Beliefs

11.1.1 Fostering Inclusivity

Respecting diverse beliefs fosters an inclusive environment where all officers feel valued and understood.

- Equal Treatment: Ensuring that all individuals are treated with respect and dignity, regardless of their religious or cultural background.

- Cultural Sensitivity: Demonstrating an awareness and appreciation of different cultural practices and traditions.

11.1.2 Building Trust and Cohesion

An inclusive approach helps build trust and cohesion within the police force.

- Trust Building: Developing trust by respecting and valuing the diverse beliefs of officers.

- Team Cohesion: Promoting a sense of unity and collaboration among officers from different backgrounds.

11.1.3 Enhancing Community Relations

Respecting diverse beliefs within the police force also enhances relations with the broader community.

- Community Trust: Building trust with diverse community groups through respectful and inclusive practices.

- Positive Interactions: Facilitating positive interactions between officers and community members from various cultural and religious backgrounds.

11.2 Challenges in Navigating Interfaith and Multicultural Dynamics

11.2.1 Conflicting Beliefs and Practices

Navigating conflicting beliefs and practices can be challenging.

- Religious Conflicts: Addressing conflicts that arise from differing religious beliefs and practices.

- Cultural Differences: Managing cultural differences that may affect communication and interaction.

11.2.2 Balancing Inclusivity and Neutrality

Balancing the need for inclusivity with the requirement for neutrality can be complex.

- Neutral Support: Providing support that is neutral and non-biased while respecting individual beliefs.

- Avoiding Favoritism: Ensuring that no particular belief system is favored over others.

11.2.3 Addressing Bias and Prejudice

Chaplains must address and mitigate any bias or prejudice within the force.

- Identifying Bias: Recognizing and addressing any personal or institutional biases.

- Promoting Tolerance: Encouraging tolerance and understanding among officers.

11.3 Strategies for Promoting Inclusivity and Understanding

11.3.1 Cultural Competency Training

Cultural competency training is essential for promoting inclusivity and understanding.

- Educational Programs: Implementing training programs that educate officers about different cultural and religious practices.

- Ongoing Learning: Encouraging continuous learning and development in cultural competency.

11.3.2 Interfaith Collaboration

Collaborating with leaders from different faith communities fosters inclusivity.

- Interfaith Dialogues: Organizing dialogues and forums with representatives from various religious communities.

- Joint Initiatives: Collaborating on community projects and events that promote mutual understanding and respect.

11.3.3 Personalized Support

Providing personalized support ensures that the needs of individuals from diverse backgrounds are met.

- Individual Assessments: Conducting assessments to understand the unique needs and preferences of each individual.

- Tailored Interventions: Designing support strategies that are personalized and culturally sensitive.

11.4 Case Studies and Real-Life Examples

11.4.1 Interfaith Prayer Service

Chaplain David organized an interfaith prayer service to honor a fallen officer, demonstrating the power of inclusivity.

- Collaborative Planning: David collaborated with leaders from various religious communities to plan the service.

- Inclusive Service: The service included prayers and rituals from multiple faith traditions, respecting and honoring the beliefs of all attendees.

- Community Impact: The inclusive approach fostered a sense of unity and respect among the diverse attendees.

11.4.2 Cultural Competency Workshop

Chaplain Maria led a cultural competency workshop for officers, highlighting the importance of understanding and respecting cultural differences.

- Workshop Content: The workshop covered various cultural practices, communication styles, and religious beliefs.

- Interactive Sessions: Maria included interactive sessions and discussions to engage officers and encourage active participation.

- Positive Outcomes: Officers reported increased cultural awareness and improved interactions with community members from different backgrounds.

11.5 Essential Qualities for Navigating Interfaith and Multicultural Dynamics

Effectively navigating interfaith and multicultural dynamics requires specific qualities and skills, including:

11.5.1 Empathy

Empathy is crucial for understanding and connecting with individuals from diverse backgrounds.

- Genuine Understanding: Demonstrating a genuine understanding and appreciation of different cultural and religious practices.

- Compassionate Support: Offering compassionate and respectful support to all individuals.

11.5.2 Cultural Competence

Cultural competence is essential for effectively navigating diverse beliefs and practices.

- Knowledge: Gaining knowledge about different cultural and religious traditions.

- Adaptability: Adapting support strategies to meet the unique needs of individuals from diverse backgrounds.

11.5.3 Communication Skills

Effective communication skills are vital for fostering inclusivity and understanding.

- Clear Communication: Communicating clearly and respectfully with individuals from diverse backgrounds.

- Active Listening: Actively listening to understand the perspectives and needs of others.

11.6 Conclusion

Respecting and accommodating diverse religious beliefs within the police force is crucial for promoting inclusivity and understanding. By fostering cultural competence, facilitating interfaith collaboration, and providing personalized support, chaplains can create a cohesive and supportive environment that values and respects diversity. Their efforts not only enhance the well-being and cohesion of the police force but also strengthen relations with the broader community.

This chapter has explored the challenges and strategies associated with navigating interfaith and multicultural dynamics, highlighting the importance of respect, empathy, and cultural competence in police chaplaincy. Subsequent chapters will delve into other aspects of police chaplaincy, including ongoing professional development and the personal rewards of serving in this essential role.

ADAPTING SERVICES TO VARIOUS CULTURAL CONTEXTS

Introduction

Adapting chaplaincy services to different cultural contexts enhances their relevance and effectiveness, ensuring that all officers feel supported. This chapter explores the importance of cultural adaptation in police chaplaincy, the challenges involved, and the strategies chaplains use to tailor their services to meet the diverse needs of the police force and the community.

11.1 The Importance of Adapting Services to Cultural Contexts

11.1.1 Enhancing Relevance

Adapting services to cultural contexts ensures that chaplaincy support is relevant and meaningful to all individuals.

- Cultural Sensitivity: Recognizing and respecting the cultural backgrounds and practices of individuals.

- Personalized Support: Providing support that is tailored to the unique cultural needs of each individual.

11.1.2 Building Trust and Engagement

Culturally adapted services build trust and encourage engagement from officers and community members.

- Trust Building: Demonstrating respect for cultural differences fosters trust and openness.

- Active Participation: Encouraging active participation by providing culturally relevant support.

11.1.3 Promoting Inclusivity

Cultural adaptation promotes inclusivity within the police force and the community.

- Inclusive Practices: Implementing practices that accommodate diverse cultural backgrounds.

- Community Relations: Enhancing relations with diverse community groups through culturally sensitive support.

11.2 Challenges in Adapting Services to Cultural Contexts

11.2.1 Understanding Diverse Cultures

Understanding the diverse cultural backgrounds of officers and community members can be challenging.

- Cultural Knowledge: Gaining comprehensive knowledge of various cultural practices and beliefs.

- Continuous Learning: Committing to continuous learning to stay informed about cultural dynamics.

11.2.2 Balancing Uniformity and Adaptation

Balancing the need for uniform chaplaincy services with the need for cultural adaptation requires careful consideration.

- Standard Procedures: Maintaining standard procedures while allowing for cultural flexibility.

- Customization: Customizing support strategies without compromising the core values of chaplaincy.

11.2.3 Addressing Cultural Sensitivities

Addressing cultural sensitivities requires a nuanced approach.

- Sensitive Topics: Navigating sensitive cultural topics with care and respect.

- Avoiding Assumptions: Avoiding assumptions and stereotypes about cultural practices.

11.3 Strategies for Adapting Services to Cultural Contexts

11.3.1 Cultural Competency Training

Cultural competency training is essential for effectively adapting chaplaincy services.

- Educational Programs: Participating in training programs that focus on cultural awareness and sensitivity.

- Practical Workshops: Engaging in practical workshops that simulate real-life cultural scenarios.

11.3.2 Building Cultural Knowledge

Building a comprehensive understanding of diverse cultural practices enhances service adaptation.

- Research and Study: Conducting research and study on various cultural traditions and beliefs.

- Community Engagement: Engaging with cultural communities to gain firsthand knowledge and insights.

11.3.3 Collaborating with Cultural Leaders

Collaborating with cultural leaders and representatives helps tailor chaplaincy services effectively.

- Community Partnerships: Forming partnerships with cultural and religious leaders to inform support strategies.

- Consultation: Consulting with cultural experts to ensure services are respectful and relevant.

11.4 Practical Applications of Cultural Adaptation

11.4.1 Tailoring Support Services

Tailoring support services to meet the cultural needs of individuals enhances their effectiveness.

- Personalized Counseling: Providing counseling that respects and incorporates cultural beliefs and practices.

- Culturally Relevant Resources: Offering resources and materials that are culturally relevant and accessible.

11.4.2 Organizing Inclusive Events

Organizing events that respect and celebrate cultural diversity promotes inclusivity.

- Cultural Celebrations: Hosting events that celebrate cultural traditions and practices.

- Interfaith Services: Organizing interfaith services that include elements from various cultural and religious backgrounds.

11.4.3 Providing Multilingual Support

Offering multilingual support ensures that language barriers do not hinder access to chaplaincy services.

- Language Resources: Providing resources and materials in multiple languages.

- Interpreter Services: Utilizing interpreter services to facilitate communication.

11.5 Case Studies and Real-Life Examples

11.5.1 Culturally Sensitive Counseling

Chaplain Emily provided culturally sensitive counseling to an officer from a different cultural background, demonstrating the importance of cultural adaptation.

- Understanding Needs: Emily took the time to understand the officer's cultural background and specific needs.

- Tailored Support: She tailored her counseling approach to incorporate cultural beliefs and practices.

- Positive Outcome: The officer felt respected and supported, leading to a positive counseling experience.

11.5.2 Organizing a Multicultural Event

Chaplain Mark organized a multicultural event to celebrate the diverse backgrounds of officers and community members.

- Event Planning: Mark collaborated with cultural leaders to plan an inclusive and respectful event.

- Cultural Activities: The event included cultural performances, food, and traditions from various backgrounds.

- Community Impact: The event fostered a sense of unity and appreciation for cultural diversity within the community.

11.6 Essential Qualities for Adapting Services

Adapting chaplaincy services to various cultural contexts requires specific qualities and skills, including:

11.6.1 Empathy

Empathy is crucial for understanding and connecting with individuals from diverse cultural backgrounds.

- Genuine Care: Demonstrating genuine care and concern for the cultural needs of individuals.

- Active Listening: Listening actively to understand cultural perspectives and experiences.

11.6.2 Cultural Competence

Cultural competence is essential for effectively adapting chaplaincy services.

- Knowledge and Understanding: Gaining knowledge and understanding of diverse cultural practices.

- Adaptability: Being adaptable and flexible in service delivery.

11.6.3 Communication Skills

Effective communication skills are vital for fostering cultural sensitivity and respect.

- Clear Communication: Communicating clearly and respectfully with individuals from diverse backgrounds.

- Multilingual Abilities: Utilizing multilingual abilities to bridge language gaps.

11.7 Conclusion

Adapting chaplaincy services to different cultural contexts enhances their relevance and effectiveness, ensuring that all officers feel supported. By fostering cultural competence, building cultural knowledge, and collaborating with cultural leaders, chaplains can create a supportive environment that respects and values diversity. These efforts not only enhance the well-being and cohesion of the police force but also strengthen relations with the broader community.

PROMOTING INCLUSIVITY WITHIN THE FORCE

Introduction

Promoting inclusivity and diversity within the police force is a key goal of police chaplaincy. By fostering an environment where all officers feel valued and respected, chaplains help create a more cohesive and supportive workplace. This chapter explores the importance of inclusivity, the challenges involved, and the strategies chaplains use to promote diversity and inclusion within the police force.

11.1 The Importance of Inclusivity in the Police Force

11.1.1 Enhancing Cohesion

Inclusivity fosters a sense of unity and cohesion among officers from diverse backgrounds.

- Teamwork: Promoting teamwork and collaboration through mutual respect and understanding.

- Shared Goals: Encouraging a collective commitment to the mission and values of the police force.

11.1.2 Improving Morale

An inclusive environment improves morale and job satisfaction among officers.

- Employee Satisfaction: Ensuring that all officers feel valued and appreciated, leading to higher job satisfaction.

- Supportive Environment: Creating a supportive work environment where officers can thrive.

11.1.3 Strengthening Community Relations

Promoting inclusivity within the police force also strengthens relations with the broader community.

- Community Trust: Building trust with diverse community groups through inclusive practices.

- Positive Interactions: Facilitating positive interactions between officers and community members from various backgrounds.

11.2 Challenges in Promoting Inclusivity

11.2.1 Overcoming Bias and Prejudice

Addressing and overcoming bias and prejudice within the force is a significant challenge.

- Implicit Bias: Recognizing and addressing implicit biases that affect interactions and decision-making.

- Cultural Sensitivity: Promoting cultural sensitivity and understanding among officers.

11.2.2 Balancing Diverse Needs

Balancing the diverse needs of officers while maintaining a cohesive force requires careful consideration.

-	Individual Needs Understanding and accommodating the unique needs of each officer.

- Equitable Practices: Implementing practices that ensure fairness and equity for all officers.

11.2.3 Ensuring Buy-In from Leadership

Gaining support and commitment from leadership is crucial for the success of inclusivity initiatives.

- Leadership Commitment: Ensuring that leadership is committed to promoting diversity and inclusion.

- Policy Implementation: Implementing policies and practices that support inclusivity at all levels.

11.3 Strategies for Promoting Inclusivity

11.3.1 Cultural Competency Training

Cultural competency training is essential for promoting inclusivity within the force.

- Educational Programs: Implementing training programs that focus on cultural awareness and sensitivity.

- Ongoing Learning: Encouraging continuous learning and development in cultural competency.

11.3.2 Inclusive Policies and Practices

Developing and implementing inclusive policies and practices fosters an environment of respect and equity.

- Diversity Policies: Creating policies that promote diversity and inclusion within the force.

- Equitable Practices: Ensuring that all practices, from recruitment to promotion, are equitable and inclusive.

11.3.3 Promoting Open Dialogue

Encouraging open dialogue about diversity and inclusion helps build understanding and respect.

- Discussion Forums: Organizing forums and discussions where officers can share their experiences and perspectives.

- Feedback Mechanisms: Implementing feedback mechanisms to gather input and address concerns related to inclusivity.

11.4 Case Studies and Real-Life Examples

11.4.1 Implementing a Diversity Training Program

Chaplain Emily led the implementation of a diversity training program that had a significant impact on the force.

- Program Development: Emily developed a comprehensive training program that included workshops, seminars, and interactive sessions.

- Officer Engagement: The program engaged officers in discussions about cultural sensitivity, bias, and inclusivity.

- Positive Outcomes: Officers reported increased cultural awareness and improved interactions with colleagues and community members.

11.4.2 Establishing an Inclusivity Task Force

Chaplain Mark established an inclusivity task force to address diversity and inclusion within the force.

- Task Force Creation: Mark formed a task force comprising officers from diverse backgrounds to address inclusivity issues.

- Action Plan: The task force developed an action plan that included policy recommendations, training initiatives, and community outreach programs.

- Enhanced Cohesion: The task force's efforts led to improved cohesion and a stronger sense of community within the force.

11.5 Essential Qualities for Promoting Inclusivity

Promoting inclusivity within the police force requires specific qualities and skills, including:

11.5.1 Empathy

Empathy is crucial for understanding and connecting with individuals from diverse backgrounds.

- Genuine Care: Demonstrating genuine care and concern for the experiences and perspectives of others.

- Active Listening: Listening actively to understand the needs and concerns of all officers.

11.5.2 Cultural Competence

Cultural competence is essential for effectively promoting inclusivity.

- Knowledge and Understanding: Gaining knowledge and understanding of diverse cultural practices.

- Adaptability: Being adaptable and flexible in service delivery.

11.5.3 Leadership

Effective leadership is vital for driving inclusivity initiatives.

- Vision: Articulating a clear vision for diversity and inclusion within the force.

- Commitment: Demonstrating a strong commitment to promoting inclusivity at all levels.

11.6 Conclusion

Promoting inclusivity and diversity within the police force is a key goal of police chaplaincy. By fostering an environment where all officers feel valued and respected, chaplains help create a more cohesive and supportive workplace. Through cultural competency training, inclusive policies and practices, and open dialogue, chaplains can effectively promote diversity and inclusion within the force.

CHAPTER 12

TRAINING AND CONTINUED EDUCATION

Importance of Ongoing Learning

Ongoing learning and professional development are essential for police chaplains to stay effective and relevant in their roles. Continuous education helps chaplains enhance their skills, stay updated with the latest practices, and address the evolving needs of the police force and the community. This chapter explores the importance of ongoing learning, the various forms of professional development, and the impact of continued education on the effectiveness of police chaplaincy.

12.1 The Importance of Ongoing Learning

12.1.1 Enhancing Skills and Knowledge

Continuous education enables chaplains to enhance their skills and knowledge, ensuring they provide the highest level of support.

- Skill Development: Developing new skills and refining existing ones to better serve the needs of officers and their families.

- Knowledge Expansion: Staying informed about the latest research, theories, and practices in chaplaincy, counseling, and related fields.

12.1.2 Adapting to Evolving Needs

The needs of the police force and the community are constantly evolving, and ongoing learning helps chaplains adapt to these changes.

- Current Issues: Addressing contemporary issues such as mental health, trauma, and diversity.

- Innovative Approaches: Learning and implementing innovative approaches to support and intervention.

12.1.3 Maintaining Professional Competence

Professional competence is essential for maintaining credibility and trust within the police force and the community.

- Ethical Standards: Adhering to ethical standards and best practices in chaplaincy.

- Accreditation: Keeping up with accreditation requirements and professional standards.

12.2 Forms of Professional Development

12.2.1 Formal Education

Pursuing formal education is a key component of professional development for police chaplains.

- Degree Programs: Enrolling in degree programs such as theology, counseling, or psychology.

- Certification Courses: Completing certification courses in specialized areas of chaplaincy and crisis intervention.

12.2.2 Workshops and Seminars

Attending workshops and seminars provides opportunities for learning and networking.

- Skill-Specific Workshops: Participating in workshops focused on specific skills such as grief counseling or crisis management.

- Professional Seminars: Attending seminars on topics relevant to police chaplaincy, such as mental health or cultural competence.

12.2.3 Online Learning

Online learning offers flexible and accessible options for continued education.

- Webinars: Joining webinars on various aspects of chaplaincy and pastoral care.

- Online Courses: Enroll in online courses offered by reputable institutions and organizations.

12.2.4 Peer Learning and Supervision

Learning from peers and supervisors is a valuable aspect of professional development.

- Peer Supervision: Participating in peer supervision groups to discuss cases and share insights.

- Mentorship: Seeking mentorship from experienced chaplains or professionals in related fields.

12.3 Key Areas for Continued Education

12.3.1 Mental Health and Counseling

Understanding mental health issues and effective counseling techniques is crucial for police chaplains.

- Trauma-Informed Care: Learning about trauma and its impact, and providing trauma-informed care.

- Crisis Counseling: Developing skills in crisis counseling to support officers during critical incidents.

12.3.2 Cultural Competence

Cultural competence is essential for providing inclusive and respectful support.

- Diversity Training: Engaging in training programs that focus on cultural awareness and sensitivity.

- Interfaith Understanding: Gaining knowledge about different religious and spiritual practices.

12.3.3 Ethical and Legal Issues

Staying informed about ethical and legal issues in chaplaincy ensures adherence to professional standards.

- Ethical Decision-Making: Learning frameworks for making ethical decisions in complex situations.

- Legal Requirements: Understanding the legal requirements and constraints related to chaplaincy.

12.4 Impact of Continued Education

12.4.1 Improved Service Delivery

Continued education leads to improved service delivery and better support for officers and their families.

- Enhanced Competence: Higher levels of competence and confidence in providing support.

- Effective Interventions: Ability to implement effective interventions and support strategies.

12.4.2 Increased Credibility and Trust

Ongoing learning enhances the credibility and trust of chaplains within the police force and the community.

- Professionalism: Demonstrating a commitment to professionalism and excellence.

- Building Trust: Building trust through knowledgeable and competent service delivery.

12.4.3 Personal and Professional Growth

Continued education contributes to the personal and professional growth of chaplains.

- Self-Development: Opportunities for self-development and personal enrichment.

- Career Advancement: Enhancing career prospects and opportunities for advancement within the field of chaplaincy.

12.5 Case Studies and Real-Life Examples

12.5.1 Pursuing Advanced Degrees

Chaplain Sarah pursued an advanced degree in counseling to enhance her skills and knowledge.

- Educational Journey: Sarah enrolled in a master's program in counseling, balancing her studies with her chaplaincy duties.

- Practical Application: She applied her new knowledge and skills to provide more effective support to officers.

- Positive Outcomes: The advanced degree improved her competence and confidence, leading to better outcomes for those she served.

12.5.2 Attending Specialized Workshops

Chaplain Mark regularly attends workshops on trauma-informed care and crisis intervention.

- Workshop Participation: Mark participates in workshops and training sessions focused on trauma and crisis management.

- Skill Enhancement: The workshops help him develop specialized skills for dealing with traumatic incidents.

- Impact on Service: Mark's enhanced skills enable him to provide better support during critical incidents, improving the well-being of officers.

12.6 Essential Qualities for Ongoing Learning

Successful ongoing learning and professional development require specific qualities and skills, including:

12.6.1 Curiosity

Curiosity drives the desire to learn and explore new knowledge.

- Lifelong Learning: Embracing the mindset of lifelong learning and continuous improvement.

- Open-Mindedness: Being open to new ideas and perspectives.

12.6.2 Commitment

Commitment to professional development is essential for sustained growth and effectiveness.

- Dedication: Demonstrating dedication to ongoing learning and self-improvement.

- Persistence: Persisting in the pursuit of knowledge and skills despite challenges.

12.6.3 Adaptability

Adaptability is crucial for applying new knowledge and skills in diverse situations.

- Flexibility: Being flexible and adaptable in implementing new approaches.

- Innovative Thinking: Embracing innovative thinking and problem-solving.

12.7 Conclusion

Ongoing learning and professional development are essential for police chaplains to stay effective and relevant in their roles. Continuous education enhances skills, adapts to evolving needs, and maintains professional competence. By pursuing formal education, attending workshops, engaging in online learning, and participating in peer supervision, chaplains can continually improve their service delivery and support for officers and their families.

AVAILABLE RESOURCES AND COURSES

Introduction

This chapter provides an overview of available resources and courses for police chaplains, helping them enhance their skills and knowledge. Access to quality educational resources and training programs is essential for ongoing professional development, enabling chaplains to provide effective support to officers and their families. This chapter explores various types of resources and courses available, highlighting their benefits and how they contribute to the growth and effectiveness of police chaplains.

12.1 Types of Educational Resources

12.1.1 Online Courses and Webinars

Online courses and webinars offer flexible and accessible learning opportunities for police chaplains.

- Flexibility: These resources allow chaplains to learn at their own pace and on their own schedule.

- Diverse Topics: Online courses cover a wide range of topics relevant to chaplaincy, such as mental health, trauma, and ethics.

- Interactive Learning: Webinars provide interactive learning experiences, often featuring expert speakers and real-time discussions.

12.1.2 Books and Publications

Books and publications are valuable resources for in-depth learning and reference.

- Foundational Texts: There are numerous foundational texts on chaplaincy, counseling, and pastoral care.

- Specialized Topics: Books covering specialized topics such as crisis intervention, grief counseling, and cultural competence.

- Journals and Articles: Academic journals and articles provide the latest research and developments in the field of chaplaincy.

12.1.3 Workshops and Seminars

Workshops and seminars offer hands-on training and networking opportunities.

- Skill Development: Workshops provide practical training in specific skills, such as conflict resolution and crisis management.

- Networking: Seminars offer opportunities to network with other professionals and share best practices.

- Expert Insights: Access to expert insights and the latest industry trends.

12.1.4 Certification Programs

Certification programs provide formal recognition of expertise and competence in specific areas.

- Professional Credentials: Earning certifications enhances professional credibility and career advancement.

- Specialized Training: Programs focused on areas such as trauma-informed care, mental health first aid, and ethical decision-making.

- Accredited Institutions: Many certifications are offered by accredited institutions, ensuring high standards of education and training.

12.2 Recommended Courses and Programs

12.2.1 Crisis Intervention and Trauma-Informed Care

Courses in crisis intervention and trauma-informed care are essential for supporting officers during critical incidents.

- Course Overview: Training on understanding trauma, its effects, and how to provide trauma-informed support.

- Provider: International Critical Incident Stress Foundation (ICISF) offers courses like "Assisting Individuals in Crisis" and "Group Crisis Intervention."

- Benefits: Enhanced ability to support officers in managing stress and trauma effectively.

12.2.2 Mental Health and Counseling

Mental health and counseling courses equip chaplains with the skills needed to address mental health issues among officers.

- Course Overview: Topics include mental health disorders, counseling techniques, and suicide prevention.

- Provider: The American Association of Christian Counselors (AACC) offers a range of courses and certifications.

- Benefits: Improved competence in providing mental health support and counseling services.

12.2.3 Cultural Competence and Diversity

Training in cultural competence and diversity is vital for promoting inclusivity within the police force.

- Course Overview: Education on cultural awareness, sensitivity, and effective communication across diverse groups.

- Provider: The National Association of Social Workers (NASW) provides courses on cultural competence.

- Benefits: Ability to provide culturally sensitive support and foster an inclusive environment.

12.2.4 Ethical and Legal Issues in Chaplaincy

Understanding ethical and legal issues is crucial for maintaining professional standards.

- Course Overview: Training on ethical decision-making, confidentiality, and legal constraints in chaplaincy.

- Provider: The Association of Professional Chaplains (APC) offers courses on ethics in chaplaincy.

- Benefits: Ensuring adherence to ethical standards and legal requirements in all aspects of chaplaincy work.

12.2.5 Pastoral Care and Spiritual Support

Courses in pastoral care and spiritual support enhance the chaplain's ability to provide comprehensive care.

- Course Overview: Topics include spiritual assessment, pastoral counseling, and providing spiritual care in diverse settings.

- Provider: The Healthcare Chaplaincy Network offers courses on pastoral care and spiritual support.

- Benefits: Strengthened skills in providing holistic care that addresses spiritual needs.

12.3 Accessing Resources and Courses

12.3.1 Online Learning Platforms

Several online platforms offer courses and resources specifically for chaplains.

- Coursera: Offers courses from top universities on topics such as psychology, counseling, and leadership.

- Udemy: Provides a variety of courses on mental health, crisis intervention, and personal development.

- edX: Features courses from renowned institutions on topics relevant to chaplaincy and pastoral care.

12.3.2 Professional Organizations

Joining professional organizations provides access to exclusive resources and training opportunities.

- Association of Professional Chaplains (APC): Offers certifications, conferences, and continuing education programs.

- International Conference of Police Chaplains (ICPC): Provides training, resources, and a supportive network for police chaplains.

- National Association of Catholic Chaplains (NACC): Offers education and certification for chaplains, with a focus on Catholic pastoral care.

12.3.3 Academic Institutions

Many academic institutions offer degree programs and continuing education courses for chaplains.

- Liberty University: Offers online degrees in divinity, pastoral counseling, and chaplaincy.

- Regent University: Provides degrees and certifications in counseling and pastoral care.

- Fuller Theological Seminary: Offers programs in theology, psychology, and intercultural studies.

12.4 The Impact of Continued Education on Chaplaincy

12.4.1 Enhanced Skills and Knowledge

Continued education equips chaplains with advanced skills and knowledge, improving their ability to serve effectively.

- Competence: Higher levels of competence in providing support and intervention.

- Expertise: Specialized knowledge in areas such as trauma, mental health, and cultural competence.

12.4.2 Increased Professional Credibility

Earning certifications and degrees enhances the professional credibility of chaplains.

- Recognition: Formal recognition of expertise and competence.

- Career Advancement: Opportunities for career growth and advancement within the field of chaplaincy.

12.4.3 Better Service Delivery

Ongoing learning leads to improved service delivery and better outcomes for officers and their families.

- Effective Interventions: Implementation of effective support strategies and interventions.

- Holistic Care: Ability to provide comprehensive care that addresses physical, emotional, and spiritual needs.

12.5 Conclusion

Access to quality educational resources and training programs is essential for the ongoing professional development of police chaplains. By engaging in continuous education, chaplains can enhance their skills, stay updated with the latest practices, and effectively address the evolving needs of the police force and the community. This chapter has provided an overview of various resources and courses available to chaplains, highlighting their benefits and impact on chaplaincy work.

Subsequent chapters will delve into other aspects of police chaplaincy, including the personal rewards of serving in this essential role and the impact of chaplaincy on the overall well-being of the police force.

STAYING UPDATED WITH BEST PRACTICES

Introduction

Staying updated with best practices ensures that police chaplains provide the highest quality of care and support to officers and their families. This chapter explores the importance of remaining current with best practices, the methods chaplains can use to stay informed, and the impact of these practices on the effectiveness of chaplaincy services.

12.1 The Importance of Staying Updated with Best Practices

12.1.1 Ensuring High-Quality Care

Adhering to best practices ensures that chaplains provide the highest quality of care.

- Standardization: Following standardized procedures and guidelines that reflect the latest research and expertise.

- Professional Competence: Maintaining a high level of professional competence and ethical standards.

12.1.2 Adapting to Changing Needs

The needs of the police force and the community are constantly evolving, and staying updated with best practices allows chaplains to adapt accordingly.

- Current Issues: Addressing contemporary issues such as mental health, trauma, and diversity.

- Innovative Approaches: Implementing innovative approaches to support and intervention.

12.1.3 Enhancing Credibility and Trust

Remaining current with best practices enhances the credibility and trust of chaplains within the police force and the community.

- Professionalism: Demonstrating a commitment to professionalism and continuous improvement.

- Building Trust: Building trust through knowledgeable and competent service delivery.

12.2 Methods for Staying Updated

12.2.1 Professional Development and Training

Engaging in ongoing professional development and training is essential for staying updated with best practices.

- Workshops and Seminars: Attending workshops and seminars on topics relevant to chaplaincy.

- Certification Programs: Completing certification programs that provide specialized training and recognition.

- Online Courses: Enrolling in online courses and webinars that offer flexibility and convenience.

12.2.2 Research and Reading

Keeping up with the latest research and literature is crucial for staying informed about best practices.

- Academic Journals: Reading academic journals and articles on chaplaincy, counseling, and related fields.

- Books and Publications: Regularly reading books and publications that cover the latest developments and theories.

- Research Databases: Utilizing research databases to access a wide range of scholarly resources.

12.2.3 Networking and Collaboration

Networking and collaborating with other professionals provide valuable opportunities for learning and sharing best practices.

- Professional Organizations: Joining professional organizations that offer resources, training, and networking opportunities.

- Peer Supervision: Participating in peer supervision groups to discuss cases and share insights.

- Mentorship: Seeking mentorship from experienced chaplains or professionals in related fields.

12.2.4 Attending Conferences

Attending conferences provides access to the latest research, trends, and best practices in chaplaincy and related fields.

- National and International Conferences: Participating in national and international conferences to learn from experts and peers.

- Specialized Conferences: Attending conferences focused on specific areas such as trauma, mental health, and cultural competence.

- Workshops and Presentations: Engaging in workshops and presentations that offer hands-on training and practical insights.

12.3 Key Areas for Best Practices in Chaplaincy

12.3.1 Mental Health and Counseling

Staying updated with best practices in mental health and counseling is crucial for effective support.

- Trauma-Informed Care: Implementing trauma-informed care practices that address the impact of trauma on individuals.

- Crisis Intervention: Utilizing best practices in crisis intervention to provide immediate and effective support during critical incidents.

- Mental Health First Aid: Applying mental health first aid techniques to recognize and respond to mental health crises.

12.3.2 Cultural Competence and Diversity

Cultural competence and diversity are essential for providing inclusive and respectful support.

- Cultural Sensitivity: Incorporating cultural sensitivity into all aspects of chaplaincy work.

- Inclusive Practices: Implementing practices that accommodate diverse cultural backgrounds and beliefs.

- Interfaith Understanding: Gaining knowledge about different religious and spiritual practices to provide appropriate support.

12.3.3 Ethical and Legal Standards

Adhering to ethical and legal standards ensures the integrity and professionalism of chaplaincy services.

- Ethical Decision-Making: Utilizing ethical decision-making frameworks to navigate complex situations.

- Confidentiality: Maintaining confidentiality and respecting privacy in all interactions.

- Legal Compliance: Understanding and complying with legal requirements and constraints related to chaplaincy.

12.4 The Impact of Best Practices on Chaplaincy

12.4.1 Improved Service Delivery

Staying updated with best practices leads to improved service delivery and better outcomes for officers and their families.

- Effective Interventions: Implementing effective support strategies and interventions.

- Holistic Care: Providing comprehensive care that addresses physical, emotional, and spiritual needs.

12.4.2 Enhanced Professional Credibility

Adhering to best practices enhances the professional credibility of chaplains within the police force and the community.

- Recognition: Formal recognition of expertise and competence through certifications and credentials.

- Career Advancement: Opportunities for career growth and advancement within the field of chaplaincy.

12.4.3 Greater Trust and Engagement

Following best practices fosters trust and engagement from officers and community members.

- Building Relationships: Building strong relationships based on trust and respect.

- Positive Outcomes: Achieving positive outcomes through knowledgeable and competent support.

12.5 Case Studies and Real-Life Examples

12.5.1 Implementing Trauma-Informed Care

Chaplain Sarah integrated trauma-informed care practices into her chaplaincy work, leading to significant improvements in support.

- Training and Certification: Sarah completed a certification program in trauma-informed care.

- Practice Implementation: She implemented trauma-informed care practices, such as creating a safe and supportive environment for officers.

- Positive Outcomes: Officers reported feeling better understood and supported, leading to improved mental health and well-being.

12.5.2 Enhancing Cultural Competence

Chaplain Mark focused on enhancing his cultural competence to better serve a diverse police force and community.

- Cultural Competence Training: Mark attended workshops and completed courses on cultural competence and diversity.

- Inclusive Practices: He implemented inclusive practices in his chaplaincy work, such as recognizing and respecting cultural holidays and traditions.

- Community Impact: The enhanced cultural competence led to stronger relationships and trust with diverse community groups.

12.6 Essential Qualities for Staying Updated with Best Practices

Staying updated with best practices requires specific qualities and skills, including:

12.6.1 Curiosity

Curiosity drives the desire to learn and explore new knowledge.

- Lifelong Learning: Embracing the mindset of lifelong learning and continuous improvement.

- Open-Mindedness: Being open to new ideas and perspectives.

12.6.2 Commitment

Commitment to professional development is essential for sustained growth and effectiveness.

- Dedication: Demonstrating dedication to ongoing learning and self-improvement.

- Persistence: Persisting in the pursuit of knowledge and skills despite challenges.

12.6.3 Adaptability

Adaptability is crucial for applying new knowledge and skills in diverse situations.

- Flexibility: Being flexible and adaptable in implementing new approaches.

- Innovative Thinking: Embracing innovative thinking and problem-solving.

12.7 Conclusion

Staying updated with best practices ensures that police chaplains provide the highest quality of care and support to officers and their families. Continuous education and professional development enhance skills, adapt to evolving needs, and maintain professional competence. By engaging in ongoing training, keeping up with research, networking with peers, and attending conferences, chaplains can effectively implement best practices and improve their service delivery.

CHAPTER 13

FUTURE OF POLICE CHAPLAINCY

Emerging Trends and Challenges

As society evolves, so too does the role of police chaplaincy. Emerging trends and challenges will shape the future of this vital role, requiring chaplains to adapt and innovate. This chapter explores these trends and challenges, providing insights into the future of police chaplaincy and the strategies chaplains can use to navigate these changes effectively.

13.1 Emerging Trends in Police Chaplaincy

13.1.1 Increased Focus on Mental Health

There is a growing recognition of the importance of mental health within law enforcement.

- Mental Health Programs: Police departments are increasingly integrating mental health programs to support officers.

- Chaplains' Role: Chaplains play a crucial role in providing mental health support, counseling, and resources to officers and their families.

13.1.2 Use of Technology

Technology is transforming how chaplains provide support and services.

- Virtual Counseling: Offering virtual counseling sessions to provide support remotely.

- Digital Resources: Utilizing digital resources and mobile apps to offer mental health and spiritual support.

- Online Training: Participating in online training and professional development to stay updated with best practices.

13.1.3 Emphasis on Diversity and Inclusion

There is an increasing emphasis on diversity and inclusion within law enforcement agencies.

- Cultural Competence: Chaplains must enhance their cultural competence to effectively support a diverse workforce.

- Inclusive Practices: Implementing inclusive practices that respect and value the diverse backgrounds of officers and community members.

13.1.4 Holistic Approach to Wellness

A holistic approach to wellness is becoming more prevalent, encompassing physical, mental, emotional, and spiritual well-being.

- Wellness Programs: Integrating wellness programs that address all aspects of well-being.

- Chaplains' Contribution: Chaplains contribute to holistic wellness by providing spiritual support and counseling, promoting mental health, and encouraging physical well-being.

13.2 Challenges in Police Chaplaincy

13.2.1 Addressing Stigma Around Mental Health

Despite progress, there is still stigma associated with seeking mental health support within law enforcement.

- Breaking the Stigma: Chaplains must work to break down barriers and encourage officers to seek help without fear of judgment.

- Creating Safe Spaces: Providing safe and confidential spaces for officers to discuss their mental health concerns.

13.2.2 Navigating Ethical and Legal Complexities

Chaplains face complex ethical and legal challenges in their work.

- Ethical Dilemmas: Navigating ethical dilemmas related to confidentiality, dual relationships, and professional boundaries.

- Legal Compliance: Ensuring compliance with legal requirements and staying informed about changes in laws and regulations affecting chaplaincy.

13.2.3 Balancing Multiple Roles

Chaplains often balance multiple roles, such as providing spiritual support, counseling, and crisis intervention.

- Role Clarity: Maintaining clear boundaries and understanding the distinct aspects of each role.

- Preventing Burnout: Implementing self-care strategies to prevent burnout and maintain personal well-being.

13.2.4 Adapting to Changing Demands

The demands on police chaplains are continually changing, requiring adaptability and flexibility.

- Evolving Needs: Responding to the evolving needs of officers and the community.

- Innovative Approaches: Adopting innovative approaches to chaplaincy that address new challenges and leverage emerging opportunities.

13.3 Strategies for Navigating Future Trends and Challenges

13.3.1 Ongoing Professional Development

Continued education and professional development are essential for staying current and effective.

Training Programs: Participating in training programs and workshops on emerging trends and best practices.

- Certification: Pursuing certifications in specialized areas such as mental health, trauma-informed care, and cultural competence.

13.3.2 Leveraging Technology

Embracing technology can enhance the effectiveness and reach of chaplaincy services.

- Telechaplaincy: Implementing telechaplaincy services to provide remote support.

- Digital Tools: Utilizing digital tools and resources to enhance support and communication.

- Online Communities: Creating online communities for peer support and resource sharing.

13.3.3 Promoting Mental Health Awareness

Chaplains can play a key role in promoting mental health awareness and reducing stigma.

- Education and Advocacy: Educating officers about the importance of mental health and advocating for mental health resources.

- Support Programs: Developing and implementing support programs that encourage officers to seek help.

13.3.4 Fostering Inclusivity

Promoting inclusivity and cultural competence is crucial for supporting a diverse police force.

- Cultural Training: Providing cultural competence training for chaplains and officers.

- Inclusive Practices: Implementing inclusive practices that respect and celebrate diversity.

- Community Engagement: Engaging with diverse community groups to build trust and understanding.

13.4 Future Opportunities in Police Chaplaincy

13.4.1 Expanding Roles and Responsibilities

The role of police chaplains is expanding to meet new challenges and opportunities.

- Specialized Support: Providing specialized support in areas such as mental health, trauma, and crisis intervention.

- Community Outreach: Enhancing community outreach efforts to build stronger relationships between law enforcement and the community.

13.4.2 Collaborative Approaches

Collaboration with other professionals and organizations can enhance the effectiveness of chaplaincy services.

- Interdisciplinary Teams: Working with interdisciplinary teams that include mental health professionals, social workers, and community leaders.

- Partnerships: Forming partnerships with local organizations, faith communities, and support groups.

13.4.3 Innovation in Service Delivery

Innovative approaches to service delivery can improve the reach and impact of chaplaincy services.

- Mobile Services: Offering mobile chaplaincy services to provide support in various locations.

- Pop-Up Clinics: Establishing pop-up clinics that offer counseling and support in different settings.

- Virtual Platforms: Utilizing virtual platforms to provide accessible and convenient support.

13.5 Case Studies and Real-Life Examples

13.5.1 Integrating Technology in Chaplaincy

Chaplain Emily successfully integrated technology into her chaplaincy work, expanding her reach and impact.

- Telechaplaincy Services: Emily implemented telechaplaincy services, offering virtual counseling sessions to officers in remote locations.

- Digital Resources: She developed digital resources, including a mental health app, to provide officers with accessible support.

- Positive Outcomes: Officers reported increased satisfaction with the flexibility and accessibility of the support services.

13.5.2 Promoting Mental Health Awareness

Chaplain Mark led a mental health awareness campaign within his police department, addressing stigma and promoting well-being.

- Awareness Workshops: Mark organized workshops to educate officers about mental health and reduce stigma.

- Peer Support Groups: He established peer support groups where officers could share their experiences and support each other.

- Improved Mental Health: The campaign resulted in increased mental health awareness and more officers seeking support.

13.6 Essential Qualities for Future Chaplains

Navigating future trends and challenges requires specific qualities and skills, including:

13.6.1 Adaptability

Adaptability is crucial for responding to changing demands and emerging trends.

- Flexibility: Being flexible and open to new approaches and ideas.

- Innovation: Embracing innovation and finding creative solutions to challenges.

13.6.2 Resilience

Resilience helps chaplains cope with the stresses and demands of their role.

- Self-Care: Prioritizing self-care and personal well-being to maintain resilience.

- Support Networks: Building strong support networks for professional and personal support.

13.6.3 Cultural Competence

Cultural competence is essential for supporting a diverse police force and community.

- Cultural Awareness: Developing an understanding of diverse cultural practices and beliefs.

- Inclusive Practices: Implementing inclusive practices that respect and celebrate diversity.

13.7 Conclusion

The future of police chaplaincy is shaped by emerging trends and challenges that require adaptability, innovation, and a commitment to ongoing learning. By staying updated with best practices, leveraging technology, promoting mental health awareness, and fostering inclusivity, chaplains can continue to provide high-quality care and support to officers and their families.

INNOVATIONS IN SUPPORT AND CARE

Introduction

Innovations in support and care are transforming police chaplaincy, offering new ways to enhance the well-being of officers and their families. These advancements provide chaplains with innovative tools and approaches to address the evolving needs of the police force. This chapter explores various innovations in support and care, highlighting their benefits and the potential they hold for the future of police chaplaincy.

13.1 Technological Advancements in Chaplaincy

13.1.1 Telechaplaincy

Telechaplaincy utilizes video conferencing and other digital platforms to provide remote support to officers.

- Virtual Counseling: Offering virtual counseling sessions to reach officers in remote locations or those who prefer online interactions.

- Accessibility: Increasing accessibility to chaplaincy services, ensuring support is available regardless of geographic barriers.

- Convenience: Providing flexible scheduling options that accommodate officers' varying shifts and responsibilities.

13.1.2 Mobile Apps and Digital Resources

Mobile apps and digital resources offer innovative ways to provide support and resources to officers and their families.

- Mental Health Apps: Developing apps that provide mental health resources, self-care tips, and crisis intervention strategies.

- Digital Libraries: Creating digital libraries with articles, videos, and other resources on mental health, spirituality, and wellness.

- Online Communities: Establishing online communities where officers can connect, share experiences, and support each other.

13.1.3 Wearable Technology

Wearable technology can help monitor and improve officers' physical and mental well-being.

- Health Monitoring: Using wearables to track physical health indicators such as heart rate, sleep patterns, and stress levels.

- Wellness Programs: Integrating wearable technology into wellness programs to provide personalized feedback and support.

- Early Intervention: Identifying early signs of stress or health issues, allowing for timely intervention and support.

13.2 Innovative Programs and Approaches

13.2.1 Peer Support Programs

Peer support programs leverage the experiences and insights of fellow officers to provide support and understanding.

- Training Peer Supporters: Training selected officers to become peer supporters who can provide emotional support and guidance.

- Support Networks: Establishing peer support networks within the department to offer continuous support.

- Confidentiality: Ensuring confidentiality to create a safe space for officers to share their concerns.

13.2.2 Holistic Wellness Programs

Holistic wellness programs address multiple aspects of well-being, including physical, mental, emotional, and spiritual health.

- Integrated Approach: Combining fitness programs, mental health support, nutrition advice, and spiritual care.

- Wellness Retreats: Organizing wellness retreats that offer comprehensive programs focused on relaxation, self-care, and personal growth.

- Mindfulness and Meditation: Incorporating mindfulness and meditation practices to help officers manage stress and enhance mental clarity.

13.2.3 Trauma-Informed Care

Trauma-informed care focuses on understanding and responding to the effects of trauma on individuals.

- Training and Education: Providing training for chaplains and officers on trauma awareness and trauma-informed practices.

- Support Strategies: Developing support strategies that recognize the impact of trauma and promote healing and recovery.

- Creating Safe Environments: Ensuring that all interactions and interventions are conducted in a manner that minimizes retraumatization.

13.3 Community-Based Innovations

13.3.1 Community Outreach and Engagement

Innovative community outreach and engagement programs build stronger relationships between the police force and the community.

- Collaborative Projects: Initiating collaborative projects with community organizations to address shared concerns and promote mutual understanding.

- Educational Workshops: Offering workshops and seminars to educate the community about the role of police chaplaincy and mental health support.

- Community Events: Hosting community events that bring officers and community members together to foster trust and cooperation.

13.3.2 Interfaith Collaboration

Interfaith collaboration leverages the strengths of various faith communities to provide comprehensive support.

- Interfaith Councils: Establishing interfaith councils that bring together leaders from different religious traditions to offer guidance and support.

- Shared Resources: Creating shared resources and programs that address the spiritual needs of a diverse police force.

- Inclusive Services: Offering inclusive spiritual services and ceremonies that respect and honor different faith traditions.

13.3.3 Volunteer Programs

Volunteer programs engage community members in supporting the well-being of officers and their families.

- Volunteer Training: Training community volunteers to provide support in areas such as peer counseling, event planning, and resource distribution.

- Mentorship Programs: Developing mentorship programs that pair officers with community mentors who can offer guidance and support.

- Resource Centers: Establishing community resource centers that provide information, support, and services to officers and their families.

13.4 Case Studies and Real-Life Examples

13.4.1 Implementing Telechaplaincy

Chaplain Emily successfully implemented telechaplaincy services to expand her reach and support.

- Virtual Sessions: Emily offered virtual counseling sessions, allowing officers to access support from any location.

- Positive Feedback: Officers appreciated the convenience and flexibility of virtual sessions, leading to increased engagement.

- Broader Impact: The implementation of telechaplaincy services resulted in greater accessibility and more timely support for officers.

13.4.2 Developing a Holistic Wellness Program

Chaplain Mark developed a holistic wellness program that addressed the comprehensive needs of officers.

- Program Components: The program included fitness training, nutrition counseling, mental health support, and spiritual care.

- Wellness Retreats: Mark organized wellness retreats that provided a space for officers to relax, recharge, and focus on their well-being.

- Enhanced Well-Being: Officers reported significant improvements in their physical, mental, and emotional health as a result of the program.

13.5 Essential Qualities for Embracing Innovation

Embracing innovation in support and care requires specific qualities and skills, including:

13.5.1 Creativity

Creativity is essential for developing and implementing innovative solutions.

- Innovative Thinking: Thinking outside the box to create new and effective support strategies.

- Problem-Solving: Using creative problem-solving skills to address challenges and improve services.

13.5.2 Adaptability

Adaptability is crucial for responding to new trends and integrating innovative practices.

- Flexibility: Being open to change and willing to try new approaches.

- Continuous Learning: Engaging in continuous learning to stay updated with the latest innovations and best practices.

13.5.3 Collaboration

Collaboration enhances the development and implementation of innovative programs.

- Teamwork: Working effectively with other professionals, community members, and organizations.

- Shared Vision: Building a shared vision for innovation and working together to achieve common goals.

13.6 Conclusion

Innovations in support and care are transforming police chaplaincy, offering new ways to enhance the well-being of officers and their families. By leveraging technological advancements, developing innovative programs, and engaging with the community, chaplains can provide more effective and comprehensive support. Embracing creativity, adaptability, and collaboration will be key to successfully navigating these innovations and ensuring the continued growth and effectiveness of police chaplaincy.

THE EVOLVING ROLE OF THE POLICE CHAPLAIN

Introduction

The role of the police chaplain is constantly evolving, adapting to the changing needs and dynamics of law enforcement and society. As the challenges faced by police officers and their families grow more complex, the scope of chaplaincy services expands to address these evolving needs. This chapter explores the factors driving the evolution of police chaplaincy, the new roles and responsibilities chaplains are taking on, and the strategies they use to remain effective in a changing environment.

13.1 Factors Driving the Evolution of Police Chaplaincy

13.1.1 Changing Social Dynamics

Social dynamics and community expectations are shifting, influencing the role of police chaplains.

- Diverse Communities: Increasing diversity within communities requires chaplains to be culturally competent and inclusive.

- Public Trust: Building and maintaining public trust in law enforcement necessitates chaplain involvement in community relations and outreach.

13.1.2 Mental Health Awareness

Growing awareness of mental health issues has heightened the need for chaplaincy services.

- Mental Health Crises: Rising mental health crises among officers highlight the need for specialized support.

- Preventative Care: Emphasizing mental health and wellness as preventative care is becoming more prevalent.

13.1.3 Technological Advancements

Technological advancements are transforming how chaplains provide support and services.

- Digital Communication: The use of digital communication tools and platforms is increasing accessibility to chaplaincy services.

- Remote Support: Telechaplaincy and virtual counseling have become integral parts of modern chaplaincy.

13.1.4 Legal and Ethical Standards

Evolving legal and ethical standards shape the practices and responsibilities of police chaplains.

- Regulatory Changes: Changes in laws and regulations impact the scope of chaplaincy services.

- Ethical Considerations: Ethical considerations around confidentiality, consent, and professional boundaries are increasingly significant.

13.2 Expanding Roles and Responsibilities

13.2.1 Mental Health Support

Providing mental health support has become a central role for police chaplains.

- Crisis Counseling: Offering crisis counseling for officers experiencing acute stress or trauma.

- Ongoing Therapy: Providing ongoing therapy and support for officers dealing with long-term mental health issues.

13.2.2 Community Engagement

Community engagement is a growing responsibility for police chaplains.

- Public Relations: Acting as a liaison between the police force and the community to build trust and foster positive relationships.

- Educational Programs: Developing and leading educational programs that promote understanding and cooperation between law enforcement and community members.

13.2.3 Diversity and Inclusion Initiatives

Chaplains are increasingly involved in promoting diversity and inclusion within the police force.

- Cultural Competency Training: Leading cultural competency training sessions for officers to enhance understanding and respect for diversity.

- Inclusive Practices: Implementing practices that ensure an inclusive environment for all officers, regardless of their background.

13.2.4 Trauma-Informed Care

Trauma-informed care is becoming a key aspect of police chaplaincy.

- Trauma Education: Educating officers about the impact of trauma and how to recognize and respond to it.

- Support Services: Providing trauma-informed support services that promote healing and resilience.

13.2.5 Technological Integration

Integrating technology into chaplaincy services is essential for meeting modern needs.

- Telechaplaincy: Offering telechaplaincy services to provide remote support and counseling.

- Digital Resources: Creating and maintaining digital resources that officers can access anytime, anywhere.

13.3 Strategies for Effective Adaptation

13.3.1 Continuous Professional Development

Ongoing professional development is crucial for staying relevant and effective.

- Advanced Training: Pursuing advanced training in areas such as mental health, trauma care, and cultural competence.

- Certifications: Earning certifications that enhance professional credentials and expertise.

13.3.2 Networking and Collaboration

Building networks and collaborating with other professionals enhances the scope and effectiveness of chaplaincy services.

- Interdisciplinary Teams: Working with interdisciplinary teams that include mental health professionals, social workers, and community leaders.

- Partnerships: Forming partnerships with local organizations and faith communities to expand resources and support.

13.3.3 Embracing Innovation

Embracing innovation is key to adapting to new challenges and opportunities.

- Innovative Programs: Developing and implementing innovative programs that address emerging needs.

- Technology Use: Leveraging technology to improve service delivery and accessibility.

13.3.4 Advocacy and Policy Involvement

Chaplains can play a role in advocacy and policy development to improve support for officers and their families.

- Policy Development: Participating in policy development processes to ensure the needs of officers are considered.

- Advocacy: Advocating for mental health resources, diversity initiatives, and supportive policies within law enforcement.

13.4 Case Studies and Real-Life Examples

13.4.1 Integrating Mental Health Services

Chaplain Emily integrated mental health services into her chaplaincy work, enhancing support for officers.

- Mental Health Training: Emily completed advanced training in mental health counseling.

- Service Implementation: She implemented mental health services, including crisis counseling and ongoing therapy.

- Positive Impact: Officers reported significant improvements in their mental health and well-being.

13.4.2 Leading Community Engagement Initiatives

Chaplain Mark led community engagement initiatives that strengthened relationships between the police force and the community.

- Public Forums: Mark organized public forums where community members could voice concerns and engage with officers.

- Educational Workshops: He developed educational workshops to promote understanding and cooperation.

- Enhanced Trust: The initiatives led to increased trust and positive interactions between the police and the community.

13.5 Essential Qualities for Evolving Chaplains

Adapting to the evolving role of police chaplaincy requires specific qualities and skills, including:

13.5.1 Adaptability

Adaptability is crucial for responding to changing needs and dynamics.

- Flexibility: Being flexible and open to new approaches and challenges.

- Continuous Learning: Engaging in continuous learning to stay updated with best practices and emerging trends.

13.5.2 Empathy

Empathy is essential for understanding and supporting officers and community members.

- Genuine Care: Demonstrating genuine care and concern for the well-being of others.

- Active Listening: Listening actively to understand the experiences and needs of those served.

13.5.3 Leadership

Effective leadership is vital for guiding and implementing change.

- Vision: Articulating a clear vision for the future of chaplaincy services.

- Inspiration: Inspiring and motivating others to embrace change and innovation.

13.6 Conclusion

The role of the police chaplain is constantly evolving, adapting to the changing needs and dynamics of law enforcement and society. By embracing mental health support, community engagement, diversity initiatives, trauma-informed care, and technological integration, chaplains can effectively meet the demands of their evolving roles. Continuous professional development, networking, innovation, and advocacy are essential strategies for staying relevant and effective.

CHAPTER 14

REFLECTIONS ON THE JOURNEY

Reflections on the Journey

Reflecting on the journey of police chaplaincy offers a deeper appreciation for its significance and impact. This final chapter encapsulates the themes discussed throughout the book, highlighting the vital role police chaplains play in supporting law enforcement officers and their families. It also reflects on the challenges faced, the strategies employed, and the ongoing evolution of this essential vocation.

14.1 The Significance of Police Chaplaincy

14.1.1 Emotional and Spiritual Support

Police chaplains provide crucial emotional and spiritual support to officers, helping them navigate the stresses and traumas of their work.

- Emotional Stability: Offering a compassionate presence and counseling during times of crisis.

- Spiritual Guidance: Providing spiritual care that aligns with the diverse beliefs of officers.

14.1.2 Building Trust and Cohesion

Chaplains foster trust and cohesion within the police force and between law enforcement and the community.

- Internal Trust: Establishing trust within the force by being a reliable source of support.

- Community Relations: Enhancing community relations through outreach and engagement initiatives.

14.2 Overcoming Challenges

14.2.1 Addressing Mental Health Stigma

One of the significant challenges has been addressing the stigma associated with mental health within law enforcement.

- Breaking Down Barriers: Encouraging officers to seek help without fear of judgment.

- Providing Resources: Offering accessible mental health resources and support.

14.2.2 Navigating Ethical and Legal Complexities

Chaplains face complex ethical and legal challenges in their work.

- Confidentiality and Consent: Maintaining confidentiality and navigating consent in sensitive situations.

- Ethical Decision-Making: Utilizing ethical frameworks to make informed decisions.

14.2.3 Balancing Multiple Roles

Chaplains often juggle multiple roles, requiring clear boundaries and self-care strategies.

- Role Clarity: Defining the distinct aspects of spiritual support, counseling, and crisis intervention.

- Preventing Burnout: Implementing self-care practices to sustain personal well-being.

14.3 Embracing Innovation

14.3.1 Technological Integration

The integration of technology has been a game-changer for police chaplaincy.

- Telechaplaincy: Offering remote support through telechaplaincy services.

- Digital Resources: Utilizing apps and online platforms to provide mental health and spiritual resources.

14.3.2 Innovative Programs

Developing innovative programs has enhanced the scope and effectiveness of chaplaincy services.

- Holistic Wellness: Implementing holistic wellness programs that address physical, mental, emotional, and spiritual well-being.

- Peer Support: Establishing peer support programs to leverage the insights of fellow officers.

14.4 The Evolving Role

14.4.1 Expanding Responsibilities

The role of police chaplains continues to expand in response to evolving needs.

- Mental Health Support: Providing specialized mental health support and crisis counseling.

- Community Engagement: Leading initiatives that foster positive relationships between the police force and the community.

14.4.2 Continuous Learning

Ongoing professional development is essential for staying relevant and effective.

- Advanced Training: Pursuing advanced training and certifications.

- Staying Informed: Keeping up with the latest research and best practices in chaplaincy.

14.5 Personal Rewards

14.5.1 Impactful Moments

The journey of a police chaplain is filled with impactful moments that highlight the importance of their work.

- Support During Crisis: Providing support during critical incidents and witnessing the positive impact on officers.

- Fostering Healing: Helping officers and their families heal from trauma and loss.

14.5.2 Professional Fulfillment

Serving as a police chaplain brings immense professional fulfillment.

- Making a Difference: Knowing that their work makes a significant difference in the lives of officers and their families.

- Personal Growth: Experiencing personal growth and development through their service.

14.6 The Future of Police Chaplaincy

14.6.1 Embracing Change

The future of police chaplaincy involves embracing change and innovation.

- Adapting to New Needs: Continuously adapting to the changing needs of law enforcement and society.

- Leveraging Technology: Utilizing technology to enhance support and accessibility.

14.6.2 Strengthening Community Bonds

Strengthening bonds between the police force and the community will remain a key focus.

- Collaborative Initiatives: Engaging in collaborative initiatives that build trust and cooperation.

- Inclusive Practices: Promoting inclusive practices that respect and celebrate diversity.

14.7 Final Reflections

Reflecting on the journey of police chaplaincy underscores its critical role in supporting law enforcement officers and their families. Through emotional and spiritual support, fostering trust and cohesion, overcoming challenges, and embracing innovation, police chaplains make a profound impact. As the role continues to evolve, chaplains will remain essential in promoting the well-being and resilience of those who serve and protect.

14.8 Conclusion

The journey of police chaplaincy is one of dedication, compassion, and continuous learning. As chaplains adapt to new challenges and embrace innovative approaches, their role becomes even more vital. This book has explored the many facets of police chaplaincy, highlighting the significance, challenges, innovations, and personal rewards associated with this essential vocation. As we look to the future, the commitment and resilience of police chaplains will continue to make a lasting difference in the lives of officers, their families, and the communities they serve.

THE LASTING IMPACT OF POLICE CHAPLAINCY

Introduction

The lasting impact of police chaplaincy is evident in the lives of officers, their families, and the community, highlighting its enduring value. This chapter reflects on the profound and lasting effects of chaplaincy, examining how it shapes the well-being of individuals, strengthens the police force, and fosters positive community relations.

14.1 Impact on Officers

14.1.1 Emotional Resilience

Police chaplains play a crucial role in building emotional resilience among officers.

- Crisis Support: Providing immediate emotional support during and after critical incidents helps officers manage stress and trauma.

- Ongoing Counseling: Regular counseling sessions promote mental health and emotional stability, enabling officers to cope better with the demands of their job.

14.1.2 Spiritual Well-Being

Chaplains address the spiritual needs of officers, fostering a sense of purpose and inner peace.

- Spiritual Guidance: Offering spiritual guidance and resources that align with the diverse beliefs of officers.

- Rituals and Ceremonies: Conducting rituals and ceremonies that provide comfort and continuity, such as weddings, funerals, and memorials.

14.1.3 Professional Development

Chaplains contribute to the professional development of officers by enhancing their coping skills and ethical awareness.

- Ethical Training: Providing training on ethical decision-making and moral reasoning.

- Stress Management: Teaching stress management techniques that improve overall job performance and satisfaction.

14.2 Impact on Families

14.2.1 Support During Crises

Families of officers receive critical support from chaplains during times of crisis.

- Grief Counseling: Offering grief counseling and support to families dealing with loss or trauma.

- Family Support Services: Providing resources and counseling to help families navigate the challenges associated with having a loved one in law enforcement.

14.2.2 Strengthening Family Bonds

Chaplains help strengthen family bonds by addressing relational issues and promoting healthy communication.

- Marriage Counseling: Offering marriage counseling and relationship support to address the unique stresses faced by law enforcement families.

- Family Workshops: Conducting workshops that focus on family dynamics, communication, and resilience.

14.2.3 Long-Term Well-Being

The long-term well-being of officers' families is enhanced through continuous support and resources.

- Resource Connection: Connecting families with community resources and support groups.

- Ongoing Check-Ins: Maintaining regular contact with families to provide ongoing emotional and spiritual support.

14.3 Impact on the Community

14.3.1 Building Trust

Chaplains play a key role in building trust between the police force and the community.

- Community Outreach: Engaging in community outreach initiatives that foster positive relationships and mutual understanding.

- Public Education: Educating the public about the role of police chaplaincy and its benefits.

14.3.2 Enhancing Cooperation

Positive relationships between the police and the community lead to enhanced cooperation and collaboration.

- Collaborative Projects: Initiating collaborative projects that address community needs and promote public safety.

- Conflict Resolution: Mediating conflicts and facilitating dialogue between community members and law enforcement.

14.3.3 Promoting Inclusivity

Chaplains promote inclusivity by respecting and celebrating the diverse backgrounds of community members.

- Cultural Competence: Leading efforts to increase cultural competence within the police force and community.

- Inclusive Practices: Implementing practices that ensure all community members feel valued and respected.

14.4 Long-Term Benefits of Chaplaincy

14.4.1 Sustainable Mental Health

The mental health benefits provided by chaplains have lasting effects on officers and their families.

- Preventative Care: Preventing mental health crises through early intervention and continuous support.

- Resilience Building: Building long-term resilience that helps individuals cope with future challenges.

14.4.2 Stronger Police Force

A supported and well-balanced police force is more effective and cohesive.

- Morale and Retention: Improving officer morale and job satisfaction, leading to higher retention rates.

- Team Cohesion: Fostering a sense of unity and teamwork within the police force.

14.4.3 Community Well-Being

The positive impact of police chaplaincy extends to the overall well-being of the community.

- Safety and Security: Enhancing public safety through improved police-community relations.

- Community Support: Providing a supportive network for community members during times of crisis.

14.5 Case Studies and Real-Life Examples

14.5.1 Supporting Officers After a Critical Incident

Chaplain Emily provided crucial support to officers following a critical incident, demonstrating the lasting impact of her work.

- Immediate Response: Emily was present at the scene, offering emotional support and counseling to affected officers.

- Follow-Up Care: She maintained regular check-ins with the officers, providing ongoing support and counseling.

- Long-Term Impact: The officers reported improved mental health and resilience, attributing their recovery to Emily's continuous support.

14.5.2 Enhancing Community Relations

Chaplain Mark's efforts in community engagement led to lasting positive changes in police-community relations.

- Community Forums: Mark organized community forums where residents could voice their concerns and engage with the police.

- Educational Programs: He developed educational programs that increased understanding and cooperation between the police and the community.

- Sustained Trust: The initiatives led to sustained trust and improved relationships between the police force and community members.

14.6 The Future of Police Chaplaincy

14.6.1 Embracing Change

The future of police chaplaincy involves continuously adapting to new challenges and opportunities.

- Innovative Practices: Implementing innovative practices that address emerging needs.

- Ongoing Learning: Engaging in continuous learning to stay updated with best practices and advancements.

14.6.2 Strengthening Impact

Chaplains can continue to strengthen their impact by focusing on key areas of growth.

- Mental Health: Prioritizing mental health support and resources.

- Community Engagement: Enhancing community engagement efforts to build stronger relationships.

- Inclusivity: Promoting inclusivity and cultural competence within the police force and the community.

14.7 Final Reflections

Reflecting on the journey of police chaplaincy reveals its profound and lasting impact on individuals, the police force, and the community. Through emotional and spiritual support, building trust and cohesion, and embracing innovation, police chaplains make a significant difference. As the role continues to evolve, the enduring value of police chaplaincy remains clear.

14.8 Conclusion

The lasting impact of police chaplaincy is evident in the lives of officers, their families, and the community. By providing emotional and spiritual support, fostering trust, and embracing change, chaplains play a crucial role in promoting the well-being and resilience of those they serve. This chapter has reflected on the significant and enduring value of police chaplaincy, highlighting its importance in maintaining a strong, cohesive, and supported police force. As we look to the future, the commitment and dedication of police chaplains will continue to make a lasting difference, ensuring their vital role remains integral to law enforcement and community well-being.

ENCOURAGEMENT FOR FUTURE CHAPLAINS

Introduction

Encouragement and guidance for future chaplains inspire the next generation to continue this important work. This chapter offers reflections, advice, and inspiration for those considering a career in police chaplaincy, highlighting the profound impact and personal rewards that come with this vital role.

14.1 The Importance of Police Chaplaincy

14.1.1 A Vital Role

Police chaplains play an essential role in supporting law enforcement officers, their families, and the community.

- Emotional Support: Providing emotional and spiritual care to officers during crises and everyday challenges.

- Building Resilience: Helping officers develop resilience and coping strategies to manage stress and trauma.

- Fostering Trust: Strengthening relationships between the police force and the community through outreach and engagement.

14.1.2 Making a Difference

The impact of police chaplaincy extends far beyond immediate support.

- Long-Term Benefits: Contributing to the long-term well-being of officers and their families.

- Community Impact: Enhancing public trust and cooperation through positive community relations.

- Personal Fulfillment: Experiencing profound personal and professional satisfaction from making a difference in others' lives.

14.2 Qualities of an Effective Police Chaplain

14.2.1 Empathy and Compassion

Empathy and compassion are fundamental qualities for a police chaplain.

- Understanding Needs: Being able to understand and respond to the emotional and spiritual needs of officers and their families.

- Showing Care: Demonstrating genuine care and concern in all interactions.

14.2.2 Adaptability

Adaptability is crucial in a dynamic and challenging environment.

- Flexibility: Being flexible and open to new approaches and changing circumstances.

- Problem-Solving: Employing creative problem-solving skills to address complex issues.

14.2.3 Strong Communication Skills

Effective communication is key to building trust and providing support.

- Active Listening: Listening actively and empathetically to understand the concerns and needs of those served.

- Clear Communication: Communicating clearly and effectively, especially in high-stress situations.

14.2.4 Integrity and Ethics

Maintaining high ethical standards is essential for credibility and trust.

- Confidentiality: Upholding confidentiality and respecting privacy in all interactions.

- Ethical Decision-Making: Making decisions based on ethical principles and professional standards.

14.3 Steps to Becoming a Police Chaplain

14.3.1 Educational Pathways

Pursuing the right education is a foundational step.

- Theological Education: Obtaining a degree in theology, divinity, or a related field.

- Counseling Skills: Developing counseling skills through additional coursework or certification programs.

14.3.2 Gaining Experience

Practical experience is invaluable for aspiring chaplains.

- Pastoral Experience: Gaining experience in pastoral care through volunteer work or internships.

- Law Enforcement Familiarity: Understanding the unique challenges faced by law enforcement through ride-along, volunteering, or related work.

14.3.3 Certification and Training

Formal certification and ongoing training are crucial.

- Chaplaincy Certification: Obtaining certification from recognized chaplaincy organizations.

- Continuous Learning: Engaging in continuous professional development to stay updated with best practices and new challenges.

14.4 Overcoming Challenges

14.4.1 Managing Stress

Being a police chaplain can be stressful; effective stress management is essential.

- Self-Care: Prioritizing self-care practices to maintain personal well-being.

- Support Networks: Building a strong support network of peers and mentors.

14.4.2 Balancing Roles

Balancing multiple roles and responsibilities requires clear boundaries.

- Role Clarity: Clearly defining and maintaining boundaries between different aspects of chaplaincy work.

- Time Management: Developing effective time management strategies to handle various responsibilities.

14.5 Inspirational Stories

14.5.1 Chaplain Emily's Journey

Chaplain Emily's story exemplifies the impact and rewards of police chaplaincy.

- Initial Challenges: Emily faced initial challenges in gaining the trust of officers but remained committed and compassionate.

- Building Trust: Through consistent support and presence, she built strong, trusting relationships with the officers.

- Long-Term Impact: Emily's dedication resulted in long-term positive changes in the mental health and well-being of the officers she served.

14.5.2 Chaplain Mark's Community Engagement

Chaplain Mark's efforts in community engagement highlight the broader impact of police chaplaincy.

- Community Outreach: Mark organized events and forums to foster positive relationships between the police and the community.

- Educational Programs: He developed programs to educate the public about the role of law enforcement and the support provided by chaplains.

- Strengthened Bonds: His work led to strengthened bonds and increased trust between the police force and community members.

14.6 The Rewards of Police Chaplaincy

14.6.1 Professional Fulfillment

Serving as a police chaplain offers profound professional fulfillment.

- Making a Difference: The knowledge that their work significantly impacts the lives of officers and their families.

- Personal Growth: Opportunities for continuous personal and professional growth.

14.6.2 Lifelong Impact

The lasting impact of chaplaincy work extends far beyond immediate support.

- Legacy of Care: Leaving a legacy of care and compassion that benefits future generations.

- Enduring Relationships: Building enduring relationships based on trust and mutual respect.

14.7 Final Words of Encouragement

14.7.1 Embrace the Journey

Embrace the journey of police chaplaincy with dedication and passion.

- Commitment to Service: Stay committed to serving officers, their families, and the community with empathy and integrity.

- Continuous Learning: Engage in continuous learning and professional development to remain effective and relevant.

14.7.2 Make a Difference

Remember that every act of support and kindness makes a difference.

- Positive Impact: Recognize the profound and lasting impact of your work on the well-being of those you serve.

- Inspire Others: Inspire others by embodying the principles of compassion, empathy, and service.

14.8 Conclusion

The journey of police chaplaincy is one of dedication, compassion, and continuous learning. Aspiring chaplains are encouraged to embrace this path, recognizing the profound impact and personal rewards it offers. By providing emotional and spiritual support, fostering trust, and embracing change, future chaplains will continue to play a vital role in promoting the well-being and resilience of law enforcement officers, their families, and the community.

APPENDICES

RESOURCES FOR FURTHER READING

Resources for Further Reading

A comprehensive list of resources for further reading provides additional insights and information on police chaplaincy. This appendix includes books, articles, websites, and organizations that can enhance understanding and support the continuous learning of current and aspiring police chaplains.

15.1 Books

15.1.1 General Chaplaincy

- "The Work of the Chaplain" by Naomi K. Paget and Janet R. McCormack

- Overview: A comprehensive guide to the various aspects of chaplaincy work, including roles, responsibilities, and best practices.

- Publisher: Judson Press

- "Hospital Chaplaincy: The Basics and Beyond" by Karen Pugliese

- Overview: Focuses on chaplaincy in a healthcare setting but offers valuable insights applicable to police chaplaincy.

- Publisher: Morehouse Publishing

15.1.2 Police and Emergency Services Chaplaincy

- "Spiritual Survival for Law Enforcement" by Cary A. Friedman

- Overview: A guide specifically for law enforcement officers, offering spiritual support and guidance to help them navigate their challenging roles.

- Publisher: Compass Books

- "Bulletproof Spirit: The First Responder's Essential Resource for Protecting and Healing Mind and Heart" by Dan Willis

- Overview: Provides practical strategies for first responders to maintain mental health and emotional well-being.

- Publisher: New World Library

15.1.3 Mental Health and Counseling

- "The Body Keeps the Score: Brain, Mind, and Body in the Healing of Trauma" by Bessel van der Kolk

- Overview: An exploration of how trauma affects the body and mind, with strategies for healing.

- Publisher: Penguin Books

- "Trauma Stewardship: An Everyday Guide to Caring for Self While Caring for Others" by Laura van Dernoot Lipsky

- Overview: A resource for those in caregiving professions, offering insights into managing secondary trauma.

- Publisher: Berrett-Koehler Publishers

15.1.4 Ethics and Professional Practice

- "Professional Spiritual & Pastoral Care: A Practical Clergy and Chaplain's Handbook" edited by Rabbi Stephen B. Roberts

- Overview: A comprehensive guide to the professional practice of chaplaincy, including ethical and legal considerations.

- Publisher: Skylight Paths Publishing

- "The Ethical Use of Touch in Psychotherapy" by Mic Hunter and Jim Struve

- Overview: Discusses the ethical considerations and best practices regarding physical touch in therapeutic settings.

- Publisher: SAGE Publications

15.2 Articles and Journals

15.2.1 Chaplaincy and Spiritual Care

- "The Role of the Chaplain in Law Enforcement" by Robert D. Hicks

- Journal: FBI Law Enforcement Bulletin

- Overview: Explores the unique role and contributions of chaplains within law enforcement agencies.

- "Spiritual Care in Crisis Situations: The Role of the Chaplain" by Peter L. French

- Journal: Journal of Pastoral Care & Counseling

- Overview: Discusses the critical role of chaplains in providing spiritual care during crises.

15.2.2 Mental Health and Trauma

- "Trauma-Informed Care in Law Enforcement" by Cheryl E. Wittenberg

- Journal: Police Chief Magazine

- Overview: An article focusing on the principles of trauma-informed care and its application within law enforcement.

- "Resilience and Coping Strategies Among Police Officers: A Review" by John M. Violanti

- Journal: International Journal of Emergency Mental Health

- Overview: A review of research on resilience and coping mechanisms used by police officers.

15.3 Websites and Online Resources

15.3.1 Professional Organizations

- International Conference of Police Chaplains (ICPC)

- Website: www.icpc4cops.org

- Overview: Provides resources, training, and support for police chaplains worldwide.

- National Association of Police Organizations (NAPO)

- Website: www.napo.org

- Overview: Offers advocacy, education, and resources for law enforcement professionals, including chaplains.

15.3.2 Mental Health Resources

- National Alliance on Mental Illness (NAMI)

- Website: www.nami.org

- Overview: Provides comprehensive resources and support for mental health issues, including crisis intervention and coping strategies.

- Mental Health First Aid

- Website: www.mentalhealthfirstaid.org

- Overview: Offers training programs designed to help individuals recognize and respond to mental health crises.

15.3.3 General Chaplaincy Resources

- Association of Professional Chaplains (APC)

- Website: www.professionalchaplains.org

- Overview: Provides certification, education, and resources for professional chaplains across various settings.

- Healthcare Chaplaincy Network

- Website: www.healthcarechaplaincy.org

- Overview: Focuses on spiritual care in healthcare settings but offers valuable resources applicable to police chaplaincy.

15.4 Training and Certification Programs

15.4.1 Chaplaincy Certification

- International Conference of Police Chaplains (ICPC) Certification

- Overview: Offers certification programs specifically for police chaplains, including basic and advanced training courses.

-   Website:
[www.icpc4cops.org/certification](http://www.icpc4cops.or
g/certification)

      - Association of Professional Chaplains (APC)
Certification

      - Overview: Provides certification for chaplains in
various settings, emphasizing professional standards and
ethical practice.

-   Website:
[www.professionalchaplains.org/certification](http://www.p
rofessionalchaplains.org/certification)

      15.4.2 Specialized Training Programs

      - Mental Health First Aid Training

      - Overview: A certification program that teaches
individuals how to identify, understand, and respond to signs
of mental illnesses and substance use disorders.

-   Website:
[www.mentalhealthfirstaid.org](http://www.mentalhealthfirs
taid.org)

      - Trauma-Informed Care Training by the Substance
Abuse and Mental Health Services Administration
(SAMHSA)

- Overview: Provides training on trauma-informed care principles and practices for professionals working with trauma-affected individuals.

- Website: www.samhsa.gov

15.5 Online Courses and Webinars

15.5.1 General Chaplaincy

- "Introduction to Chaplaincy" by Coursera

- Overview: An online course covering the basics of chaplaincy, including roles, responsibilities, and best practices.

- Website: www.coursera.org

- "Spiritual Care and Counseling" by edX

- Overview: Offers an in-depth look at providing spiritual care and counseling in various settings.

- Website: www.edx.org

15.5.2 Mental Health and Trauma

- "Psychological First Aid" by Johns Hopkins University on Coursera

- Overview: A course designed to teach the principles of psychological first aid and its application in crisis situations.

- Website: www.coursera.org

- "Trauma-Informed Care" by FutureLearn

- Overview: An online course that explores the principles and practices of trauma-informed care.

- Website: www.futurelearn.com

Conclusion

This comprehensive list of resources provides additional insights and information on police chaplaincy, supporting the continuous learning and professional development of current and aspiring chaplains. By exploring these books, articles, websites, and training programs, chaplains can enhance their knowledge, skills, and effectiveness in their vital roles. This appendix serves as a valuable guide for those committed to the ongoing journey of providing compassionate and professional support to law enforcement officers, their families, and the community.

CONTACT INFORMATION FOR CHAPLAINCY ORGANIZATIONS

Introduction

Connecting with chaplaincy organizations is essential for aspiring chaplains to access valuable networks, resources, and support systems. This chapter provides contact information for key chaplaincy organizations, offering guidance on how to engage with these entities to enhance professional development and effectiveness in police chaplaincy.

15.1 National and International Chaplaincy Organizations

15.1.1 International Conference of Police Chaplains (ICPC)

- Website: www.icpc4cops.org

- Address: 2424 W Brandon Blvd 116, Brandon, FL 33511, USA

- Phone: +1 (813) 784-4411

- Email: info@icpc4cops.org

- Overview: ICPC provides training, certification, and support for police chaplains worldwide. Their programs focus on enhancing the skills and knowledge necessary for effective chaplaincy in law enforcement settings.

15.1.2 National Association of Police Organizations (NAPO)

- Website: www.napo.org

- Address: 317 S. Patrick Street, Alexandria, VA 22314, USA

- Phone: +1 (703) 549-0775

- Email: info@napo.org

- Overview: NAPO offers advocacy, education, and resources for law enforcement professionals, including chaplains. They work to support the needs and well-being of police officers across the United States.

15.1.3 Association of Professional Chaplains (APC)

- Website: www.professionalchaplains.org

- Address: 1701 E. Woodfield Road, Suite 400, Schaumburg, IL 60173, USA

- Phone: +1 (847) 240-1014

- Email: info@professionalchaplains.org

- Overview: APC provides certification, education, and resources for chaplains in various settings. They emphasize professional standards and ethical practice in chaplaincy.

15.1.4 Federation of Fire Chaplains (FFC)

- Website: www.firechaplains.org

- Address: PO Box 223202, Princeville, HI 96722, USA

- Phone: +1 (808) 826-3919

- Email: info@firechaplains.org

- Overview: FFC supports chaplains serving fire departments and emergency services. They offer training and resources tailored to the unique challenges of fire and emergency service chaplaincy.

15.2 Specialized Chaplaincy Organizations

15.2.1 Law Enforcement Chaplaincy Foundation (LECF)

- Website: www.lecf.org

- Address: 1430 Alhambra Blvd, Suite 102, Sacramento, CA 95816, USA

- Phone: +1 (916) 978-0296

- Email: info@lecf.org

- Overview: LECF provides training, resources, and support for law enforcement chaplains. They focus on building resilient and effective chaplaincy programs within police departments.

15.2.2 International Network of Prison Ministries (INPM)

- Website: www.prisonministry.net

- Address: PO Box 230, Somerville, TX 77879, USA

- Phone: +1 (409) 775-3998

- Email: info@prisonministry.net

- Overview: INPM supports chaplains and ministries serving prison populations. They offer resources and networking opportunities for those involved in correctional chaplaincy.

15.2.3 National Organization for Victim Assistance (NOVA)

- Website: www.trynova.org

- Address: 510 King Street, Suite 424, Alexandria, VA 22314, USA

- Phone: +1 (703) 535-6682

- Email: info@trynova.org

- Overview: NOVA provides training and resources for chaplains and professionals working with victims of crime. They focus on enhancing the support and advocacy provided to victims and their families.

15.3 Faith-Based Chaplaincy Organizations

15.3.1 National Association of Catholic Chaplains (NACC)

- Website: www.nacc.org

- Address: 4915 S. Howell Avenue, Suite 501, Milwaukee, WI 53207, USA

- Phone: +1 (414) 483-4898

- Email: info@nacc.org

- Overview: NACC provides certification, education, and support for Catholic chaplains. They emphasize the integration of faith and professional practice in chaplaincy.

15.3.2 Healthcare Chaplaincy Network (HCCN)

- Website: www.healthcarechaplaincy.org

- Address: 505 Eighth Avenue, Suite 900, New York, NY 10018, USA

- Phone: +1 (212) 644-1111

- Email: info@healthcarechaplaincy.org

- Overview: HCCN supports chaplains in healthcare settings, providing resources and training applicable to various chaplaincy contexts, including law enforcement.

15.3.3 The Church of England Chaplaincy Network

- Website: www.churchofengland.org

- Address: Church House, Great Smith Street, London SW1P 3AZ, United Kingdom

- Phone: +44 20 7898 1000

- Email: comms@churchofengland.org

- Overview: The Church of England offers resources and support for chaplains serving in various sectors, including law enforcement. They provide training and networking opportunities for Anglican chaplains.

15.4 Online Chaplaincy Communities and Forums

15.4.1 Chaplaincy Innovation Lab

- Website: www.chaplaincyinnovation.org

- Overview: An online community and resource center dedicated to the advancement of chaplaincy across different fields. They offer webinars, research, and networking opportunities.

15.4.2 The Chaplain Hub

- Website: www.chaplainhub.com

- Overview: An online forum for chaplains to share experiences, resources, and support. The platform facilitates discussions on best practices, challenges, and innovations in chaplaincy.

15.4.3 Spiritual Care Association (SCA)

- Website: [www.spiritualcareassociation.org](http://www.spiritualcarea ssociation.org)

- Overview: SCA offers a comprehensive online platform for chaplains, providing access to training programs, certification, and a global community of spiritual care providers.

Conclusion

Connecting with chaplaincy organizations provides aspiring and current chaplains with access to valuable networks, resources, and support systems. The contact information provided in this chapter serves as a guide for engaging with these organizations, enhancing professional development, and ensuring effective chaplaincy services. By leveraging these resources, chaplains can continue to grow in their roles, making a lasting impact on law enforcement officers, their families, and the community.

SAMPLE FORMS AND DOCUMENTS

Introduction

Sample forms and documents provide practical tools and templates for police chaplains to use in their work. This chapter includes various forms and documents that can assist chaplains in their daily responsibilities, ensuring they have the necessary resources to perform their duties effectively and efficiently. These samples can be adapted to fit specific departmental needs and regulations.

15.1 **Confidentiality Agreement**

Confidentiality Agreement for Police Chaplaincy

Police Department: _______________________________

Chaplain Name: _______________________________

Effective Date: _______________________________

Purpose:

This agreement outlines the confidentiality obligations of the police chaplain in relation to the information shared by officers, their families, and other members of the police department.

Agreement:

1. Confidentiality: The chaplain agrees to keep all information shared by officers, their families, and other department members confidential, except in cases where disclosure is required by law or with the explicit consent of the individual.

2. Record Keeping: The chaplain agrees to maintain any records securely and ensure that they are only accessible to authorized personnel.

3. Disclosure: The chaplain agrees to inform individuals of any limitations to confidentiality, particularly in cases involving harm to self or others.

4. Duration: This confidentiality agreement remains in effect indefinitely, even after the chaplain's service with the police department ends.

Signatures:

Chaplain Signature: _______________________________

Date: _______________________________

Police Chief Signature: _______________________________

Date: _______________________________

15.2 **Incident Report Form**

Police Chaplaincy Incident Report Form

Police Department: _______________________________

Date of Incident: _______________________________

Time of Incident: _______________________________

Location of Incident: _______________________________

Officer(s) Involved: _______________________________

Chaplain Name: _______________________________

Description of Incident:

____

____

____

____

____

____

Actions Taken:

____

____

____

____

____

____

Follow-Up Required:

____

____

____

____

____

Signatures:

Chaplain Signature: ________________________________

Date: __________________________

Supervisor Signature: ______________________________

Date: __________________________

15.3 Counseling Session Notes

Counseling Session Notes

Date: _________________________

Time: _________________________

Officer Name: _________________________

Chaplain Name: _________________________

Summary of Session:

____

____

____

____

____

____

Key Issues Discussed:

____

____

____

____

____

Action Plan/Recommendations:

____

____

____

____

____

____

Next Session Date:

____

____

Signatures:

Chaplain Signature: _______________________________

Date: _______________________________

Officer Signature: _______________________________

Date: _______________________________

15.4 **Referral Form**

Referral Form for External Services

Police Department: _______________________________

Date: _______________________________

Officer Name: _______________________________

Chaplain Name: _______________________________

Reason for Referral:

____

____

____

____

____

____

Referred To:

Organization/Service: ___________________________

Contact Person: ___________________________

Address: ___________________________

Phone Number: ___________________________

Email: ___________________________

Additional Information:

____

____

____

____

____

____

Signatures:

Chaplain Signature: ___________________________

Date: ___________________________

Officer Signature: ___________________________

Date: ___________________________

15.5 **Crisis Intervention Checklist**

Crisis Intervention Checklist

Police Department: _______________________________

Chaplain Name: _______________________________

Date: _______________________________

Immediate Actions:

- [ ] Ensure the safety of all individuals involved.

- [ ] Assess the immediate needs of the individual(s).

- [ ] Provide emotional support and reassurance.

- [ ] Contact additional support services if needed (e.g., medical, psychological).

- [ ] Document the incident and actions taken.

Support Provided:

- [ ] Emotional support

- [ ] Spiritual support

- [ ] Crisis counseling

- [ ] Referral to external services

- [ ] Follow-up plan established

Follow-Up Actions:

- [] Schedule follow-up session with the individual(s).

- [] Communicate with relevant support services.

- [ ] Monitor the individual(s) progress and provide ongoing support.

- [] Update records with all relevant information.

Signatures:

Chaplain Signature: _______________________________

Date: _______________________________

Supervisor Signature: _______________________________

Date: _______________________________

15.6 Chaplaincy Program Evaluation Form

Chaplaincy Program Evaluation Form

Police Department: _______________________________

Evaluation Period: _______________________________

Chaplain Name: _______________________________

Program Components:

1. Emotional and Spiritual Support:

    -    Quality   of   counseling   sessions: _______________________________

- Availability and accessibility: ___________________________

- Officer satisfaction: ___________________________

2. Community Engagement:

- Effectiveness of outreach programs: ___________________________

- Community feedback: ___________________________

- Engagement levels: ___________________________

3. Training and Professional Development:

- Participation in training sessions: ___________________________

- Relevance and quality of training: ___________________________

- Impact on chaplain performance: ___________________________

4. Crisis Intervention:

- Response time: ___________________________

- Effectiveness of intervention: ___________________________

- Follow-up support: ___________________________

Overall Program Effectiveness:

____

____

____

____

____

Recommendations for Improvement:

____

____

____

____

____

Signatures:

Evaluator Signature: _______________________

Date: _______________________

Chaplain Signature: _______________________

Date: _______________________

The sample forms and documents provided in this chapter serve as practical tools and templates for police chaplains. By utilizing these resources, chaplains can ensure they are well-equipped to handle various aspects of their role, from confidentiality agreements and incident reports to counseling notes and program evaluations. These templates can be customized to meet the specific needs of different departments and help streamline chaplaincy operations, ultimately enhancing the support provided to officers, their families, and the community.

INDEX

A detailed index helps readers quickly locate specific topics and information within the book. This index is organized alphabetically by key terms and concepts discussed throughout the chapters.